KT-520-204

Tony Morrison is a zoologist, film maker and writer. During the past seventeen years he has explored remote parts of South America, especially the deserts of the Andes, to search for rare wildlife. He is a member of the Flamingo Survival Group of the I.C.B.P. of the Smithsonian Institution. The research for this book has grown from many expeditions made with his wife, who (at the same time as travelling with two small children) has taken many of the photographs. Their previous work includes *Land Above the Clouds*, a book about Andean wildlife, *The Andes* for Time-Life Books, and numerous television films, including *Mystery on the Desert*, made in 1963, and *Pathways to the Gods*.

Dr Gerald S. Hawkins is a physicist, astronomer and science writer. From 1962 to 1974 he was a staff member of the Smithsonian Institution. In 1968 he made the first professional ground and air survey of the Nasca desert lines. The air-survey plans, reproduced in this book, are a unique record of these fast-disappearing features of the desert, and form the basis of the astronomical conclusions derived by computer study.

Also by Tony Morrison

The Andes
Land Above the Clouds

Tony Morrison

Pathways to the Gods

The Mystery of the Andes Lines

and incorporating the work of
Gerald S. Hawkins

PALADIN
GRANADA PUBLISHING
London Toronto Sydney New York

Published by Granada Publishing Limited
in Paladin Books 1980

ISBN 0 586 08346 4

First published in Great Britain by
Michael Russell (Publishing) Ltd 1978
Copyright © Tony Morrison 1978

Granada Publishing Limited
Frogmore, St Albans, Herts AL2 2NF
and
3 Upper James Street, London WIR 4BP
866 United Nations Plaza, New York, NY 10017, USA
117 York Street, Sydney, NSW 2000 Australia
100 Skyway Avenue, Rexdale, Ontario, M9W 3A6, Canada
PO Box 84165, Greenside, 2034 Johannesburg, South Africa
CML Centre, Queen & Wyndham, Auckland 1, New Zealand

Filmset in 'Monophoto' Ehrhardt 10 on 12 pt and
printed in Great Britain by
Fletcher & Son Ltd, Norwich

This book is sold subject to the condition that it
shall not, by way of trade or otherwise, be lent,
resold, hired out or otherwise circulated
without the publisher's prior consent in any
form of binding or cover other than that in
which it is published and without a similar
condition including this condition being imposed
on the subsequent purchaser.

Granada ®
Granada Publishing ®

Contents

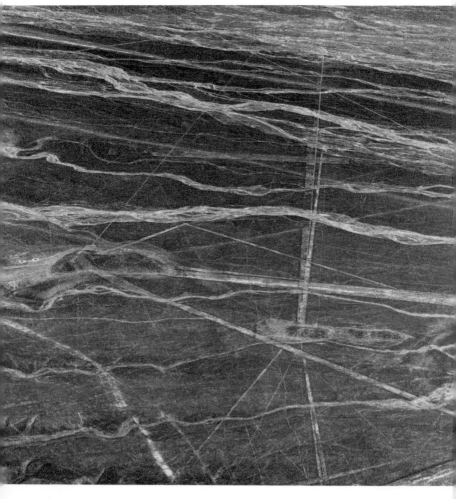

Preface

That the Nasca lines were the work of ancient man is a point of contact between many theories. As a zoologist I was intrigued by the animal designs drawn among the lines and as a film maker my curiosity was heightened by conversations with Maria Reiche who has lived and worked in the Nasca desert for over thirty years. Her determined enthusiasm has gained her worldwide admiration and this was recognized by the Peruvian Government when, in September 1977, it conferred on her the Order of Merit 'for forty years of study and dedication to the lines of Nasca'. Maria Reiche and her sister, Dr Renate Reiche-Grösse, must have first claim for my thanks.

The work of Dr Gerald S. Hawkins has been incorporated extensively within this book and I am indebted to him for permission to use many maps and diagrams. Such an association might have been impossible had it not been for the late Paul Johnstone, executive producer of the BBC series, 'Chronicle', which recorded Dr Hawkins's Nasca survey on film.

It was with Dr Hawkins's report and with new information gathered from several expeditions that I turned to television to co-sponsor a longer and far wider investigation. I would like to thank Bayerischer Rundfunk, Munich, and the 'Chronicle' team for a decision to attempt to film a philosophy widely believed to be an impossible subject for television.

At an early meeting, Dr Warwick Bray, Dr Peter Francis, Olivia Harris and John Hemming gave opinions I value greatly. I have appreciated discussions and correspondence with the late Professor Jacob Bronowski, Dr Chávez Ballón, Dr Roland Hamilton, Dr Patricia Lyon, Carlos Ponce Sanginés, Dr Patricia Netherly, María Rostworowski de Diez Canseco, Professor John Rowe and Dr Tom Zuidema. I also thank the organizations and friends mentioned in 'Acknowledgements'. My special thanks must go to Heather Sherlock, editor-in-chief; to Duncan Masson as an explorer and discoverer of many desert lines; to Richard

Brinckerhoff for help with computing; to Peter and Wendy Williams without whom the book would never have been written; and particularly to my wife Marion, who has travelled across many of the remoter parts of South America and whose work on the planning of our expeditions, and in the field, is incalculable.

Tony Morrison

Lines and the shape of a giant bird on the Nasca desert.

Straight lines lead over hills above the Palpa valley.

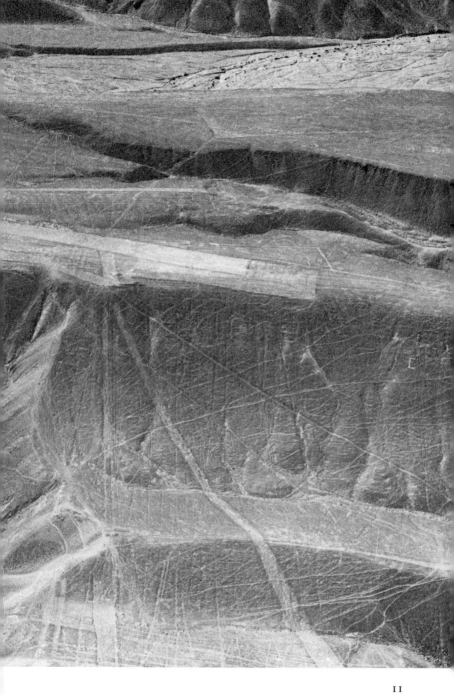

A two-dimensional zoo rests between the lines of Nasca.

1 A Desert Mystery

The glowing desert below the wingtip of our plane was a network of lines and crazy patterns stretching for miles to the horizon. One line slid into the viewfinder of my camera, perfectly straight as if it had been made by some dextrous giant – some supergod. It led into more lines which formed a narrow triangle, like a strange runway. More absolutely true lines were followed by others depicting figures – a beautifully expressive bird, a monkey fleeing; then another triangle, a huge rectangle and a double spiral. Some lines led straight as arrows over dry riverbeds and hills. Others converged on hummocks like cart-wheel-spokes on a hub. Beside the large rectangle a switchback-like pattern of thin parallel lines lay as neatly as tracks in a railway shunting yard. I kept shooting pictures as we circled again and flew back once more over the desert to look at South America's most amazing archaeological mystery.

Who had made these extraordinary markings and why? They were cut into the virgin desert pavement, and their purpose just as their exact age, was unknown. Etched into this arid area of coastal Peru by hands now forgotten, centuries or even millennia ago, their variety seemed limitless. As the Peruvian Air Force pilot turned back to the dirt landing strip at Nasca, I realized I was lost to the puzzle of the lines: their age, their meaning and the people and culture that had spawned and created them.

That was in 1963 when I was making a film for the BBC 'Adventure' series. It was not the first time I had been to the site. A year and a half earlier I had passed through Nasca on the last but one leg of a round-the-world expedition with Mark Howell, a fellow explorer. In the deserts of the Middle East we had been fascinated by the relics of civilizations that had flourished long before the time of Christ. But that was history we had learned at school. South America, and especially Peru, was part of a mysterious new world where most of the visible remains were younger than the great cathedrals of Europe. Yet the details of the Nasca culture were lost in the dust, unrecorded. Why should this be so?

Probably the answer lay in the restrictive policies of the Spanish Crown which effectively sealed off its newly gained South American colonies from the rest of the world until the late eighteenth century. Even today some of the more remote and inhospitable parts of the continent remain unexplored.

Mark and I had been shown air photographs of the lines when we first reached Peru. When we tried to locate the markings on the ground, however, we found them unexpectedly indistinct. It soon became clear that the scale was so large that they could only be appreciated from the air. Who was meant to view them?

Months later back in London, Brian Branston, a Yorkshireman and TV producer, was looking over the shoulder of a film editor in the Ealing film studios. One of the large rectangles appeared on a tiny screen.

'It looks like a landing ground. Why didn't you get a shot as if you were approaching for touch down?' A joking remark he meant half seriously. I had to admit that such a use had never occurred to me. It has occurred to others since.

Immense clearings and lines made long ago in the western foothills of the Peruvian Andes.

The animal drawings at Nasca drew comparisons with other far-flung sites. Branston asked if I knew of the legendary Zodiac of Glastonbury – the astrological bestiary believed to exist as mounds in the flat plain of Somerset in the west of England? Or could there be a connection, in concept at least, between the Nasca drawings and hill figures in Britain, or mounds in the deserts of America? The mystery haunted me, and in the following years of travelling to study wildlife in South America I visited Nasca many times – nineteen visits between 1961 and 1977 – and gradually sifted the clues.

On the second occasion, in 1963, I met Maria Reiche, a German mathematician who at that time was completing her seventeenth year of living on the desert. She outlined her theory that the lines led directly to the rising and setting points of celestial bodies on the horizon. She said then that 'the ancients believed there was some mysterious significance in the way one star would set below one horizon and another star would appear in the opposite direction'. The Nasca desert had earlier been described as 'the largest astronomy book in the world' by Dr Paul Kosok, a history professor of Long Island University. In 1941, when studying ancient irrigation there, he had seen the sun setting at the end of a line on 22 June, the mid-winter solstice in Peru.

By 1968 this thesis had been checked by Dr Gerald S. Hawkins, the Boston-based Smithsonian astronomer who had just proposed some

remarkable astronomical knowledge for the builders of Stonehenge in southern England. I was with his survey team in Peru that year to film his work for 'Chronicle', the BBC archaeological programme. His discovery was soon to gain general acceptance and lead to the new fields of astroarchaeology and archaeoastronomy. His exact computer investigations were later to cast some insight into the Kosok-Reiche theory.

Also in 1968 came the first of the sensational suggestions proposing some extraterrestrial significance. A landing ground for U.F.O.s? Did U.F.O.s exist? Had 'little green men' visited Nasca? Could that be the answer?

There was only one certain piece of evidence. The Nasca lines did not stand alone. Lines in different forms exist as a Pan-Andean phenomenon and many authorities in South America, knowing of my interest, have pointed to numerous other sites. At one of these, on a high plateau 450 miles from Nasca, were signs that the lines were still in use by the mountain Indians. Here at last would be an opportunity to ask questions: to probe into the mind of the indigenous people of the Andes and thus conceivably solve the mystery.

Although the use would not be defined with certainty, I began my search in the hope that even if the purpose had been forgotten, not every trace would have been erased by the passage of time. If I could find sufficient clues I might possibly piece together a plausible explanation. This was my aim. My first objective was to establish the recent history of the Nasca lines. Who had discovered them? How and when? I had completed all the research I could do in Britain, Spain and the United States; now I needed to make another expedition to Peru.

The Pan-American Highway crosses ancient markings only a few miles from Nasca.

Arid land borders the Pacific for about 2,000 miles.

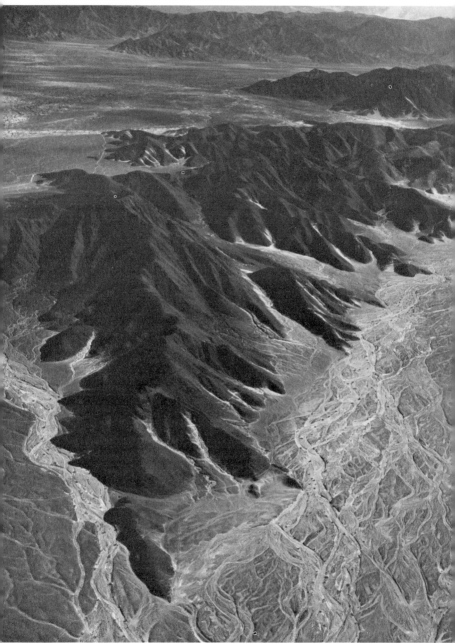

River Jequetepeque

Cajamarca

Trujillo

River Virú

Casma

Andes

Collique San Damián
Lima Huarochirí
River Lurín
Pachacámac

Chincha

Paracas
Peninsular

Ica

Machu Picchu

Tambo Machay
Cuzco
Mt Ausangate
20.939 (feet)

Pan American
highway

Nasca Puquio
Marcona
River Yauca
Yauca

Lake Titicaca

Puno

Guaqui **La Paz**
Arequipa

Tiwanaku

River Desaguadero

Pacific

Mt Sajama
21.390 (feet)

Chile

19

The Nascas

The Nasca culture is recognized through the products of people who lived in a large part of the south coast of Peru between 1,400 and 2,350 years ago. The Nascas, however, were not the first to inhabit the area: dated sites confirm that the central Andes were occupied sometime between 9,000 and 12,000 years ago. Apparently the first hunters' descendants gradually settled there, cultivated plants, developed pottery and, later, weaving, and used maize. As powerful religious traditions grew, ceremonial centres and temples were built which have withstood the passage of time in the arid desert landscape. Kahuachi, a shrine of the Nascas, stands on the south side of the Nasca river and comprises six pyramids, or natural hills faced with tall wedge-shaped adobes. The highest mound rises more than 65 feet and overlooks a walled court of 4,050 square yards. Clearly associated with Kahuachi, the Estaquería was a strange array of 120 log pillars (once 12 rows of 20), now much reduced by local charcoal burners.

The Estaquería.

The Nascas deformed the heads of children.

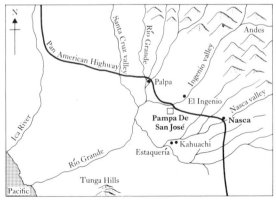

20

A feather mantle from a Nasca grave.

Nasca pottery.

Over a thousand years of
infrequent rainstorms have
destroyed the upper levels of the
courts and pyramids of
Kahuachi.

Santiago de La Nasca from a drawing by Felipe Guamán Poma, a seventeenth-century
Indian artist.
Burials were simple. Urns were used occasionally in later graves.

The road to Nasca skirts the dry foothills of the Andes to cross well-irrigated valleys, once the home of the Nasca people. The town itself is some twenty-five miles away (to the right).

The shrine of Pachacámac overlooks the sea.

2 The Lines of Nasca

Christmas 1976 was two days away when I landed at Jorge Chavez airport on the outskirts of Lima. Now the modern Peruvian capital, it was founded by Francisco Pizarro, the *conquistador*, at the foot of the Andes over four centuries ago. I hired a Volkswagen and headed south along the asphalted Pan-American Highway, following the Pacific coast-line through an extraordinary lunar-like desert landscape. The Highway is modern, though it is not the first to be there. The Incas, a predominantly highland civilization, built a road along the coast to link the river valleys. The custom in those days was to establish posts or stopping-places where runners known as *chasquis* halted to pass on messages or goods to the next man.

This narrow strip, about 1,800 miles in length, squeezed between the cloud-wreathed Andes and the Pacific, is one of the driest places on earth. A uniquely cold Pacific swell rolls against the shore of steep cliffs and sterile canyons and, further inland, the on-shore winds suck the landscape dry. Some fifty-three rivers cross this desert from the Andes to the sea, creating ribbons of green on the otherwise stone-strewn plain. The landscape is changeless; should you tread on the desert or drive your car over it, your mark will remain for centuries. More important, this dryness and changelessness has preserved intact many remains of pre-Columbian civilization. As I was to see, some relics, like the Nasca lines, can still tell a story in a land where an ancient written language was unknown.

Fifteen miles south from Lima, I reached the adobe ruins of Pach-acámac, an ancient ceremonial centre dedicated to a creator god and the most significant of all the Inca works to be built on the coast. Originally an important site used by earlier cultures, Pachacámac was en-larged by the Incas in the second half of the fifteenth century when they conquered the coastal people and advanced into their territory. Infrequent rainstorms over 500 years have destroyed the site only superficially. It mostly resembles a vast irregular mound, yet where

Duncan Masson began exploring the Peruvian desert when he was seventeen. His first car, a Model T Ford, was fitted with a Rucksell rear axle, giving it four speeds forward and two reverse – ideal for desert work.

archaeologists have cleared the covering layers, perfect adobe walls, some still with original colouring, are exposed. In fact, millions of handmade mud bricks form a pyramid or sun temple seventy-five feet high on a base extending over twelve acres, built in homage to ancient gods.

Ica, 193 miles on, is a bustling town of mainly single-storey buildings designed for safety in an area where earth tremors are a recurring hazard. It was summer and the wide streets were lined with orange-flowering acacia trees. I had arranged to meet Duncan Masson, a retired Scot whose father had been an industrial chemist working oil milled from cotton seeds grown in the Ica valley. As a young man straight from school, Duncan crossed the desert many times, often in his Model T Ford. He held the forty-eighth driving licence issued in Ica. In those days there was no road to Lima. The choice was simple: blaze the trail over the harsh desert or travel by sea.

Duncan became a desert explorer and in the following years amassed an unequalled knowledge of the Ica region. He was heavily tanned from years of outdoor life, broad-shouldered and with a purposeful walk. Slightly suspicious at first, he looked at me through his small dark-rimmed spectacles.

'I heard you were coming via the bush telegraph. It's Nasca you're

Pan American-Grace Airways – Panagra – operated the Ford Trimotor on the South American routes. The arrival of this aircraft, the *San José*, at the Tinguiña airfield, Ica, in the early 1930s was a memorable event.

interested in, isn't it? I was working on the Hacienda Las Mercedes down there in 1929.'

We shook hands.

'Come on in.'

He led me into his low, white-painted house, and prepared a jug of ice cold *refresco* – freshly pressed juice of limes with water. He told me he had driven over the lines quite frequently in the early thirties, on his way from the hacienda to Nasca twenty-five miles away. Like many other travellers, he had believed they were ancient roads.

'I saw them first in 1928. We passed them in the desert. They are very clear when you look along them; otherwise, as you know, they're almost invisible.'

Archaeologists had first noticed the lines when an expedition to the Nasca desert was led by Julio C. Tello, a highly respected pioneer of modern Peruvian archaeology. Tello, accompanied by three friends, was digging a site at Cantallo, near Nasca, in September 1926. Late one afternoon, taking advantage of the low angle of the sun, two of his team, Mejía Xesspe, a Peruvian, and Alfred Kroeber, an American, climbed a hill in search of more ruins. Instead they noticed the desert markings and duly recorded them.

By the early 1930s, the lines had been well known also to the pilots

Even the frequent sandstorms have not obliterated the markings on the hills of Los Piscontes.

of the Peruvian Air Force, and of the two private companies that operated regular passenger services in the area. Faucett, the second oldest airline in South America, is Peruvian, and Panagra, using the Ford Trimotor, a huge plane in those days, also flew Lima to Arequipa in the south of the country. These aircraft refuelled at a rough strip in Ica, and Duncan knew many of the pilots, including Elmer J. Faucett, the American founder of the famous company.

I left the shade of Duncan Masson's house to head south to Nasca eighty-five miles away.

'You'll find lines as soon as you leave this valley,' he said. 'Look on the hills to the left once the road starts to climb.' Thanking him, I turned back to the car and the implacable heat.

The Pan-American Highway led south down the Ica valley through well-ordered vineyards and cotton fields. Once away from Ica, the road was either fenced or lined with barriers of large opuntias, or prickly pear cacti, native to the Americas. I drove slowly through several villages with houses of mud and cane until eventually a sign pointed to Ocucaje, a well-known Peruvian vineyard. It was at this sign that the rich green valley once more gave way to sandy desert. I quickly recognized the low hills Duncan had mentioned.

I stopped the car and walked across the sand. A thin wedge-shape marked the side of the hill where it had been cleared of stones, extending from the flat general level of the desert right up to the summit. Using a compass I made a rough check of the azimuth (the compass bearing in degrees counted east from north). It was 260 degrees. So I had spotted Los Piscontes, sometimes called Los Retamales and named after a local bush like broom. A second hill nearby had two clear lines leading to the top. Without climbing the hills there was no chance of learning more, but as they were so close to the valley and the marks were likely to have been disturbed, I concluded I should press on to Nasca.

Nasca lies some thirty-eight miles from the coast where the desert strip has its greatest width. To reach it the road climbs slowly before plunging into a short tunnel through a spur of grey-pink mountains. At the far end of the tunnel I blinked in the sunlight to see a deep valley spread out below and beyond it the level plateau of the Nasca desert as a line on the horizon, fourteen miles away.

The rocky *pampas* of Río Grande.

From my vantage-point, I looked across the valley to a closer and somewhat lower plateau. A very obvious trapezoidal marking had been made there. It was the first of the familiar 'Nasca' patterns. The road descended sharply to the Río Grande and continued south across flat beds of a grey conglomerate scoured from the Andes sometime between one million and ten thousand years ago. Two small tributaries of the Río Grande, the Palpa and Ingenio, had eroded deep gullies in the curiously rounded hills. Lines that included even modern political graffiti stood out clearly on almost every hillside. Green fields flanked a narrow bridge crossing the Ingenio River and the way ahead was an easy climb between long tongues of rocky deposits. In less than two minutes I arrived on a broad plateau. To the east the Andes rose abruptly and to the west the distance was lost in a shimmering haze. This was the Pampa de San José, *pampa* being an old South American word meaning 'flat place'. The *pampa* in front of me was empty and virtually flat apart from a gentle rise to the south where an isolated group of low hills interrupted the skyline.

Nothing seemed to have changed greatly in the sixteen years since my first visit, except that an adobe bar-restaurant that had once stood at the roadside had been demolished. The dusty stump of a single palm tree remained and two features were new: signboards declaring the

pampa a protected archaeological site, and a tall metal observation tower erected a few steps from the road.

I pulled off the highway and stopped behind a buff Toyota with local registration plates. The occupants were clambering up the steps to the viewing platform. A guard in charge of the tower proffered a visitors' book for me to sign. I searched for some change.

'How much to go up?'

'Nothing, *señor*, the *Doctora* says it's free.'

That would be typical of Maria Reiche, I thought, to build a tower near the lines so that visitors endeavouring to locate the markings would not harm the surface of the *pampa*. She once told me how she had found footsteps made by Dr Kosok in 1941, their clarity undimmed by the passing years.

I joined the group at the top of the tower. On the *pampa* to the east the lines were too distant to be clear. However, by turning to the other side of the tower our climb was rewarded: six parallel lines pointed in a north-westerly direction and, reaching almost to the foot of the tower, stretched the outline of a giant hand or seaweed-like marking. The tourists, all Peruvians, had seen the drawings more clearly that morning from a small Cessna and we talked about the curiously invisible nature of the drawings from the ground.

Seen close at hand it was apparent that the lines had been constructed by clearing the stony surface of the *pampa* to reveal the fine light-coloured dust beneath, which over the years had been turned a purplish-brown colour by desert varnish. Where cars had been driven over the desert, they left behind tracks of a brilliant pale yellow. In ancient times the drawings must have stood out equally conspicuously and their current obscurity must be in part due to their antiquity. The Pampa de San José – basically a rocky desert pavement – presents an ideal surface for marking patterns.

The great concentration of Nasca drawings is on this *pampa* within two miles of the observation tower. It includes the monkey, spider, humming bird and condor, as well as flowers, hands and spirals – altogether more than thirty pictures and even more spiral designs, varying in size from a few feet to over 600 feet from end to end. On the flat surface of the desert they are as much a part of the mystery as the lines themselves; and they too can be seen only from the sky. Without some kind of airship – and no archaeological evidence supports the airship theory – the original creators would never have seen the magnificence of their finished work. And magnificent it surely is. Each drawing is made as a single, narrow, continuous line and the Nascas must have possessed great skill and dedication to project their thoughts like this on to the stony canvas of the desert. Time was probably of no consequence and the local manpower fairly easily organized; but artistically some of the drawings are quite remarkable.

Paul Kosok and his wife first discovered the Nasca drawings in June 1941. Dr Kosok said that at that time the remains of the huge pebble and dirt drawings were faint, and the designs when plotted on paper 'reminded me somewhat of the pictures on the Nasca pottery'. Indeed, some figures do resemble the animal and angular designs painted on the pottery, and the remainder, including the strange convoluted plants and hands, could represent other mythological spirits or even visions of the Nascas. Kosok suspected that the animal drawings were ritual paths. Of the other drawings, most of the human figures are scraped on sloping hillsides and can be seen from ground level.

By 1948, when Kosok and his son Michael visited Nasca, Maria Reiche had located a further eighteen figures, some of which Kosok cleaned by dragging a stone on a rope behind him as he shuffled along the lines in heavy boots! Other paths have since been brushed clean and now show clearly from the air. But they darken again after a few years as the wind exposes darker, heavier particles and pebbles. The *pampa*

Paul Kosok, a native New Yorker and one time conductor of the Brooklyn Civic Orchestra, was a man of many talents – archaeologist, historian, physicist and musician. After travelling to India and China, he turned to the archaeology of Peru where he investigated ancient irrigation systems.

does perhaps have a claim to be 'the world's largest scratch pad', as one of my companions on an earlier expedition somewhat flippantly described it.

Yet the question remained. Why cover the *pampa* with lines and drawings, and why with lines so meticulously straight that the deviation according to Gerald S. Hawkins is less than four yards in a mile? Surely this precision points to a purpose of some significance. The most likely builders would be the ancient people of the Ingenio valley one third of a mile away. Why did they need or want these lines?

At the foot of the observation tower, I asked the guard for news of Maria Reiche. His reply confirmed she was still hard at work, her dedication undimmed. That morning she had left the *pampa* early and driven her Volkswagen into Nasca, another fifteen miles south. 'A brown Combi, *señor*. Look in the garage of the Turistas Hotel.'

I located Maria Reiche in the shaded garden of the hotel. She was sitting alone beside the swimming pool, working at the problem that was her life, her notes on the table beside her. She was dressed in a cotton shirt and grey trousers. Her back was still as straight, her face deeply tanned beneath her almost white hair. She had altered little since I first met her in the days when she went camping on the desolate

Maria Reiche has dedicated the greater part of her adult life to studying the desert markings of Nasca. She began her work in earnest during the summer of 1946, fourteen years after her first visit to Peru. A room in the Hacienda San Pablo at Ingenio near Nasca was Maria Reiche's field headquarters and 'home' for almost thirty years. She now lives in Nasca.

pampa, sometimes for weeks on end. She had been almost sixty then, and though the recent years had imposed a certain outward frailty, I soon realized that her mathematical mind was as crisp as ever. We had last met in London when she attended the opening of an exhibition of Nasca photographs. There she had seemed tired and ill at ease. Here in Nasca she was alive, vibrant. She was 'at home'.

I tried hard to keep the discussion to lines, but her involvement with her most recent work on the animal figures was irrepressible. She had calculated an ancient unit of measurement which she believed those lost ancient people used when they planned the figures. Like some other early measuring units, she said, the Nasca unit had been derived from a standard taken from the length of a human arm. (Historical records reveal that Inca culture, too, included a system of measurement units derived from the human body.) Her time in recent years has been absorbed in deducing a method of construction for the figures. The most likely procedure seems to have included a small scale model, and she has discovered such a model and even some fragments of what she

identified as red and white chalk on the ground. She suggested that the ground would have been used by the Nascas rather like a blackboard for the preliminary design. Then, by use of cords and a factor to enlarge the scale, the design could have been transferred to another position on the *pampa* in the size they are seen today.

When I met Maria Reiche for the first time she had already been on the *pampa* for seventeen years. By 1977 she had completed another fourteen. I asked her why she had stayed in Nasca. Her answer was simple.

'I was very impressed with the vastness of the *pampa*, the solitude.' She paused. 'I love solitude.'

She spoke perfect English with only a slight hint of a German inflection. Her father had been a judge who died in World War 1. She studied mathematics and geography in Hamburg and Dresden where she took her final degree. Though she first visited Peru in 1932, it was not until 1939 and 1940 that she got to know Paul Kosok who was studying ancient irrigation methods along the coast. After Kosok had visited the Nasca *pampa* in 1941, *Life* magazine published some of his photographs together with his theory that the markings formed the largest astronomy book in the world. Maria Reiche was inspired by Kosok to investigate the ancient astronomy he believed to be the explanation of the lines.

The Pan-American Highway had been built by the time she began, and making her base in an old hotel in Nasca she went to the desert at 4 a.m. each day with the trucks and early buses, so avoiding the worst of the dazzling heat. She explained how, by starting from the highway, she would walk into the open desert, following a line. She was greatly intrigued by instances where a number of lines converged. Early in her investigation she found the figure of a spider, and after that she documented more lines, figures and the large cleared spaces. She describes the clearings, which are probably the most obvious features from the air, as triangles and quadrangles, and believes that both the shapes and the dimensions had a special significance to the ancient people that made them. She went on to say that she had measured the widths of certain rectangular surfaces and found they had similar measurements of slightly over sixty-six yards. Possibly the builders had used measuring ropes carried from place to place and handed down from generation to generation, so that a standard measurement could have been maintained for a long period.

To explore the desert, Maria Reiche has lived for days and sometimes weeks away from her Ingenio H.Q. Often she walks alone or crosses the pebbly wasteland in a jeep or Volkswagen.

I returned to a theme we had touched on in January 1963 and enlarged upon many times since. The astronomical theory. Her views?

'The ancient people thought that a star which rose in the east came from a house which contained the star which set in the west directly opposite it.' In this way the lines linked the rising and setting points on the horizon.

Using a star chart given to her by Paul Kosok, she had spent years calculating all the rising and setting points of stars in relation to the direction of the lines – or the edges of large cleared features. And her conclusion was that a great number of lines and triangles coincided with the rising and setting points of the group of stars known as the Pleiades, or 'Seven Sisters'.

Among my notes were pictures I had shot in 1963 – aerial views of a site close to the edge of the Nasca valley. A wide triangle pointed to a hill. The tiny figure standing by a pick-up truck was Maria Reiche.

'Do you recognize your camp?' I asked.

She raised her spectacles and held the photograph close to her eyes. 'Yes, yes of course, but you mustn't say exactly where it is or it will be spoiled by the visitors. The very wide triangle dates from very early times and the little triangle beside it at the north-east dates from 1400 B.C.' She paused thoughtfully. 'So many people come here now since

Author Tony Morrison and Maria Reiche in 1977.

that spaceman story.' Clearly the vulnerability of the lines concerned her deeply.

We ordered a drink. For Maria Reiche a fresh grapefruit juice mixed with milk. 'Will he know how to make it?' I asked as the waiter walked away – I had a nasty image of curdled milk.

'Yes. Of course. He knows me well.' She smiled as she spoke, a gentle reminder that she had been in Nasca for more than thirty years.

I asked for a large bottle of cold, *bien helada*, Arequipeña, a fine beer from southern Peru.

'Which do you think has the greatest significance – the spirals, animals, lines or cleared areas?'

Her answer was concise. 'The lines, animals and spirals in that order. The cleared areas are really associated with lines and so are of no prime importance.'

As always, her enthusiasm made her astronomical theories exciting. People at tables around us turned to listen. They were welcome to eavesdrop. I recalled the evening back in London when she had held the rapt attention of a packed audience at the Institute of Contemporary Arts. There she had said the lines were the basis of an agricultural calendar. They had been marked out in ancient times under the direction of specialists, possibly priests. At one place on the *pampa* she had found a small centre containing four solstice lines, two equinox lines and one line for the mid-point between solstice and equinox, the 'eighth of the year'. One of these would have indicated a date near 6 May, which in the Andes is harvest time.

By using the lines to predict the positions of celestial objects, the astronomer priests could determine the times of the year for planting, or the annual appearance of the water in the rivers (due to rains in the high mountain valleys sixteen miles distant), together with the festivals that marked these important events. At her London lecture Maria Reiche had said she believed that the lines might also have been used to predict eclipses. No record of such sophistication in native astronomy was recorded by the Spanish chroniclers after the conquest, but, she said, the Spaniards denied their conquered peoples all semblance of cultural values 'apparently to justify their pillage'.

As Maria Reiche continued her explanation, I reflected on the many occasions we had met on the *pampa*. In the early days she had been given the use of a tiny adobe room in a farm building owned by Lyndon Evelyn, an Englishman and manager of the Hacienda San Pablo in the Ingenio valley only nine miles from where Duncan Masson had also worked. Here the desert was at her door. She had only to cross the road and climb a bank to the *pampa*, using the same route as the line builders might have used countless centuries before. In fact she had spent the most productive years of her life living and sleeping in the open on the *pampa*, existing on a meagre diet of fruit and nuts while measuring and recording lines, literally hundreds of lines.

'Why,' I asked, 'did the ancient people make so many of these lines?'

'It is to do with precession,' she replied.

As we look into space there is an apparent surface of the heavens on which the stars appear to be fixed. For convenience this is named 'the celestial sphere'. Precession is the apparent movement of constellations – about one degree per century – that is produced by a gradual change in the direction of the earth's axis of rotation. A period of precession is completed every 26,000 years when the stars regain the position on the sphere that they held at the beginning of the period. Maria Reiche said that fifty years was sufficient to cause a noticeable difference in the position of some stars. She suggested that this movement of the stars would surely have been observed by the ancient astronomers and that when a star no longer rose or set at the end of a line, the people built another accurate line in the new position. This, Maria Reiche believes, might account for the many lines that occur around one centre or observation point.

I felt I had to mention the work carried out by Gerald Hawkins who in 1968, with a team of scientists and surveyors, had made an accurate plan of lines on the Pampa de San José. A computer check had found no significant correlation between the lines and positions of any stars at any conceivable date in antiquity. Yet Maria Reiche was as firm as ever in her conviction that her calculations provided proof. She did not doubt the accuracy of the computer but claimed the sample was 'inadequate', adding that the numbers the machine produced referred to the wrong lines. But she did not explain to what, specifically, the 'wrong lines' pointed.

Later I thought over our conversation. In her thirty-one years on the *pampa*, Maria Reiche has painstakingly measured and calculated dates for many of the lines, but has published few details. I believe that until such time as those details are published the calendar theory cannot be thoroughly checked and substantiated. Science demands that any idea must be aired and discussed.

The book that Maria Reiche published in 1949, *Mystery on the Desert*, is a remarkable book but it was written at the beginning of her investigations and contains no firm conclusions. It is, however, a most valuable document for its observations of the Nasca site before tourists and cars destroyed some of the features. It contains many valuable clues. At that time, for example, locals remembered wooden posts standing at the ends of some lines but these have since been taken away and used by the farmers as firewood.

What are the facts? What is the historical record? My interest was primarily lines, straight lines and particularly those lines crossing hills and gullies without deviation. I hoped that by comparing evidence of other line sites in the Andes which I would explore later, the meaning of the straight lines, calendric or otherwise, would become obvious. I have tremendous respect for the hardy Spaniards who slogged across unknown South America recording in minute detail as they went. In sixteen years of travelling in remote parts of the Andes, I have seldom encountered a region that had eluded them four centuries ago. I was optimistic that my search deep in the Spanish archives would be rewarded.

Here I was to be disappointed however. There were no early records of Nasca, due apparently to the disordered state of the coastal people at the time of the conquest in 1532. They had only recently been absorbed into the Inca empire, when an outbreak of a plague, probably brought by the earliest Spanish invaders, drastically reduced their numbers. Wars followed between Francisco Pizarro's half brother, Gonzalo, and the Spanish Crown, in which hundreds of Indians lost their lives. Within fifty years of Pizarro's landing, the southern coast population was virtually wiped out. According to one contemporary chronicler writing in the sixteenth century, 'Of the 30,000 people who lived in the valley of Chincha [just north of Nasca] only 600, or a little more, now were alive.' Most of the important chroniclers, particularly those concerned with religion and local beliefs, began writing fifty years after the conquest and naturally had little reason to visit an uninhabited land. Perhaps one day an obscure reference may be located in a so far undiscovered chronicle, but the odds seem much against it.

Mejía Xesspe, the Peruvian archaeologist, referred me to a chronicle by Luis de Monzón, the *corregidor* or magistrate of Rucanas and Soras near Nasca in 1586. He had described an ancient people 'before the Incas' . . . 'who built roads that are visible today, as wide as a street' (presumably a narrow sixteenth-century street). It is just possible that the Nasca lines were used as roads, but I was intrigued by certain details in Maria Reiche's book which indicated otherwise. I needed to go once again to the Nasca *pampa* and attempt a visual reconstruction of the appearance of the lines as they were made, to gain some insight into the original motive for building them. The desert had been a quiet place in 1961, but now, sixteen years later, only a remote corner of the *pampa* would retain the isolation, the solitude cherished by Maria Reiche. It was late afternoon when I set out beyond the town of Nasca itself.

There was little chance of discovering a line or triangle totally unvisited by local treasure-hunters and tourists but I walked hopefully along the edge of a valley fringed by tough mimosas and spiny opuntias. A small green humming bird darted swiftly from a flower and hovered inquisitively in front of me. Then the change from fertile valley to desert was abrupt: a matter of a good stride from the green fields to the pebbly waste of the *pampa*.

The climb to the plateau was easy. I followed a narrow twisting path, remembering to place one foot carefully in front of the other to avoid unnecessarily disturbing the stones. Maria Reiche had insisted on this rigorous procedure from the moment we had first met. The level of the open *pampa* was no more than seventy feet above the valley and with the low angle of the sun the ancient markings were easily visible. I had reached the broadest end of a long trapezoidal clearing. The surface had been diligently cleared centuries before and the stones placed in regular piles and set in rows that were distinguishable across the length and breadth of the area.

The cleared surface was delineated by a low border of heaped stones and earth. A layer of finely fragmented oxidized rock covered the cleared ground, possibly blown there from the desert, or oxidized *in situ* after the clearing work had been done. At the broad end of the clearing overlooking the valley, in an approximately southerly direction, I found three large heaps of stones. One had been crudely dismantled by treasure-hunters, but the others were perfect.

These stone piles, or mounds, are features described by Maria Reiche in her book. They are large, two feet high and often six to ten feet in diameter, and each with a shallow depression at the top. The depressions are filled with sand. Maria Reiche suggested that the wooden posts once seen on the *pampa* could have stood in the stone mounds. I examined the mounds in detail. They were mostly sited at the end of lines or in the extremities of the cleared areas in places which might have been significant to the builders. I had found similar stone piles or *apacitas* in the Andes built recently by Indians at places they venerated.

I searched carefully around the mounds. The first was nothing more than an apparently random pile of surface stones from the *pampa*. At the next pile I had better luck: much of the heap seemed to be built from rocks larger than the surface material. Some of the pieces were eight to twelve inches in diameter and clearly rounded by water or glacial action. The builders could have carried them there from the valley or a gully about a hundred yards away.

Padre Rossel Castro, a priest in Nasca in the 1940s, observed that in those days the mounds were believed to be tombs and local *huaqueros* (or treasure-hunters) expected to find pottery in them. Rossel Castro discovered bones of small animals in the soil-filled depressions of some mounds. Perhaps these were sacrificial remains? Or maybe they were no more than the remains of an errant desert fox? Maria Reiche wrote that sea shells were common in places she later explained as prehistoric camping sites marked by stones. Had she meant stone piles? Cairns?

What was the significance of the cairns? Could they be markers set up to fix precise alignments of a feature to a celestial body? Or viewing positions used by the ancient astronomers? Places like that would have

Long rows of stone piles were arranged in many of the cleared areas. This trapezoid is near the Nasca valley.

been sacred to the ancient people. Blood offerings were also common in ancient times and the chroniclers described them. I had seen that these were still made in the Andes. Also, offerings of sea shells are made usually at springs or in other places in the hope of bringing rain or water.

I followed a track which passed along the cleared trapezoid. It was recent and not straight; a mule trail probably. The clearing was uniform and the small heaps of stones were arranged in two main rows, one each side of the centre. The order of these could simply represent the number of people employed in the construction. Apart from the neatly arranged heaps the trapezoid contained nothing. But where it reached a junction with the border of another cleared area I noticed three fragments of ceramic: the beautifully decorated pottery of a style archaeologists attribute to the Nasca culture, a recognizable and distinctive product of the people who once inhabited a large part of the southern coast of Peru.

The ceramic was not unexpected. In 1949 Maria Reiche had recorded how several vessels were found intact upside down at the intersection of two cleared areas. Another vessel was found with two stones on top of a mound, also at an intersection, and Maria Reiche concluded that they were not funeral pots but perhaps associated with some 'unknown' ritual. Other unexplained artefacts found on the lines were stones with designs. One bore a snake's head and a small trophy. Others had rings of dark yellow and light brown. It is arguable that these might have been produced with the natural pigments used by the Nasca pottery craftsmen.

Young Josue Lancho with pieces of broken Nasca pottery. Where the pottery is found the fragments are very numerous.

An unexpected patch of grey caught my eye. As I bent down I saw a small mouse lodged between surface stones. It was dead and very dry, its tiny body shrivelled yet perfect in every detail. There was no way of determining how long it had lain there as a mummified corpse. Nothing changes in the desert. Yet the absence of human remains seems curious. No observer has recorded finding burials right out on the *pampa* among the lines: the cemeteries of the ancient people are found mostly in the desert close to the valley walls, just above the fertile ground.

I remembered that in the 1940s an eminent Peruvian historian, Dr Hans Horkheimer, noticed a large number of lines connecting what he described as 'burials' to the cleared areas. He termed the latter *plazoletas*, or small squares – as you find in a village. Dr Horkheimer concluded that the areas had been associated with an ancestor cult marked by gatherings of descendants who held dancing rituals in the cleared spaces. Maria Reiche, too, suggested the possible ritual or religious use of the clearings and of the stone mounds.

I continued along the trapezoid until I reached a line which seemed to stretch endlessly into the *pampa*. After following it for almost sixty yards I reached a low pile of stones. The stones might well have been taken from the surface of the *pampa* nearby though individually they were larger than most I could see there. Stepping over the pile, I walked on, and in roughly another sixty yards I found a similar pile. Maria Reiche had said that these piles on or beside a line were common and highly significant. She did not elaborate. It was only later, back in Nasca, that I got more clues on these stones. I met Josue Lancho, a

Stone piles built centuries ago are common features among the lines.

schoolmaster, member of the Nasca Council and director of the town museum. He had a simple and seemingly logical explanation.

The *Municipalidad*, or Town Hall, is on one side of the central *plaza* in Nasca. The tiny museum stands to the right. A young girl with brown eyes and a bright smile dispensed a ticket for ten *soles* (the equivalent of seven cents).

'Is the director here?' I asked hesitantly.

'*Si* . . . Doctor Lancho . . .,' and she turned to one of two Peruvians in deep discussion a few feet away.

I introduced myself and Josue Lancho in turn introduced me to Alberto Garcia, the town's mayor. We shook hands. I explained my interest in the lines and told them the BBC was planning to make a film later in the year.

'Anything you need, let us know,' Señor Garcia offered immediately. 'And Doctor Lancho will help you with the lines – he has his own views,' he added with a grin. 'Don't you, Josue?'

We shook hands again and he left us.

Josue Lancho had all the local theories at his fingertips. His approach was to seek the simplest answer. He pointed to rows of ancient pots.

'Wonderful designs, you see. Excellent craftsmen, yet their life was simple. Why look for anything complicated?'

We talked for two hours during which he outlined his theory of the methods used by the ancients to make the lines. They could have used three poles or just two if a distant sighting point was involved. One pole would need to be held at the starting mark and the middle pole, held perhaps one hundred yards away, would be moved from side to side until an observer at the first pole could see the middle pole and distant mark in alignment. The tops of the poles might have been sharpened to increase the accuracy of sighting.

Josue Lancho later arranged a demonstration of this technique for our BBC film crew. His team of schoolboy surveyors set out their poles and, having aligned them, piled stones around the bases to keep them upright. They used cords to form the lines between the poles. When they removed their poles after the job had been done, small heaps of stones remained at regular intervals down the centres of the lines. If Josue Lancho was correct, the piles of stones I had seen on the *pampa* would indicate that this method had been employed centuries earlier.

I queried the basis for his explanation. Had any special poles been discovered in the graves? Or the cords? It was common to find the belongings of a person buried with him.

'No, no special poles are known though there is plenty of *cane*' (a *Gynerium* species) 'in the valley. It's the type used in the houses. They could have used that.'

'The cords?'

'No, again nothing special, but if you want to lay bricks or dig any trench, a cord is the simplest way of keeping it straight.' They had found plenty of string and balls of cotton in the graves.

We agreed to meet after lunch for an excursion. When I arrived at the *plaza* in my hire car, Josue Lancho was waiting with his nine-year-old son, Josue, nicknamed 'Cholo' to avoid confusion. They jumped in and directed me to the outskirts of the town where we turned off the main road on to a track. At the foot of a mountain spur they pointed to a parking place. As we left the car, father shouted to son that he should leave the pottery alone. He turned to me, explaining with a laugh: 'Cholo will make a good *huaquero* if the police don't stop him!'

Evidently this was not the first time Cholo had been there. While I followed his father up a steep slope, Cholo walked into the desert. From our viewpoint a broad level fill of grey conglomerate spread between the Andean foothills. A large trapezoid had been cleared and through it ran a zigzag line leading to a large spiral at one end.

'We call this the needle and ball of wool.'

Cholo had reached the join of spiral and line.

'*Oye*, Cholo, start now,' shouted Josue. The boy ran carefully around the spiral, quickly reaching the centre. Then he resumed, running along the same single line path in the desert.

'There, I believe the lines were for ritual dances . . . and look at those stone mounds.'

He pointed to large heaps of stones similar to those I had seen on the *pampa*. The heaps were sited at the corners of each angle of the zigzag.

'As they danced they would pass these mounds. They would have made offerings at the stones – they do that in the mountains even now.'

He waited for my opinion and commented, 'There's plenty of broken pottery near those heaps.'

Certainly his simplistic view was attractive. Should straight lines need complicated mathematics to explain them?

As we clambered down the hill and returned to the car, I was aware of two important considerations. It was clear that several local experts

Nasca children used simple methods to build a line in the desert beside their school.

could suggest entirely plausible motives for line building and these they supported by reference to surviving customs and the known tradition of the ancient people. On the other hand, hard evidence was lacking and without it even the most detailed theory would remain conjecture.

That evening I left Nasca and headed back towards Ica in the hope that Duncan Masson could answer some of the puzzles in my mind. The setting sun was veiled by thin cloud and by the time I had reached the Pampa de San José it was almost dark.

Behind me, to my right, the Andes were covered by heavy summer rain clouds and lightning flashed silently in the mountains. The *pampa* lay mysteriously deserted. What of the thousands of ancient Nascas labouring to clear their ritual *plazas*? Might they have processed along the lines carrying lighted torches, or jars of offerings for libations with ritual sacrifices? Was I probing too deep for their ancient gods?

A splash of rain hit the windscreen: quickly it blurred and I stopped to fit the wiper blades thoughtfully hidden in the glove pocket by the hire firm. Rain drops are rare and magical in that place. On my first visit with Maria Reiche, in 1963, a sudden shower had stopped us at the same point on the road. Would the ancient Nascas have needed a calendar to warn them of the changing seasons? And could it have been based on astronomy? Several years earlier astronomer Gerald Hawkins had visited Nasca to look into that possibility.

The strange alignments at Nasca caught the attention of Gerald S. Hawkins in 1968. With a team of Peruvian surveyors, he examined the linear features on the Pampa de San José.

Many of the lines were so straight that the deviation was less than four yards in a mile.

3 Calendars and Computers

Behind the crossed hairlines of the theodolite, the alternate red and white bands of a ranging pole glistened in the desert heat of the Pampa de San José. It was July 1968 and I lifted my head from the instrument's telescope to face a group of scientists and surveyors gathered in a semicircle waiting for my comment. This international group had come to Nasca with a grant from the National Geographic Society to put some scientific muscle into solving the mystery of the desert lines, and I was to film them for the BBC.

As I turned to speak, the tenths of a degree I had visually recorded from the theodolite a second before blanked totally from my memory. I was suddenly struck by stage fright and I could muster no more than: 'That shimmer . . . can it affect the result?'

The sturdy, cleanshaven man in a white golfer's hat, standing beside me, hand in his red cotton jacket, was Dr Gerald Hawkins, leader of the group. An astronomer with the Smithsonian Astrophysical Observatory, he had achieved controversial acclaim when in 1963 he published his work on Stonehenge, which, he had said, functioned as a neolithic sun and moon observatory. Maybe, even, a computer.

'It has no effect, Tony, not over that distance,' he responded in a crisp transatlantic way and, turning to one of the Peruvian surveyors, added: 'Anyhow Professor Salas has said he'll be making a double check at this site tomorrow.'

Gerald Hawkins spoke earnestly to the professor and then made a few calculations on a slide rule: in those days pocket calculators were yet to be developed. His computer was 4,000 miles away, in Cambridge, Massachusetts. Then he scribbled a quick back-of-the-envelope calculation while we waited with breathless expectation.

'Well,' – a slight pause, then a thoughtful glance at the paper and then at the line. 'Well, I don't think we're going to find out yet, but if Steve can fix a long distance phone link, we'll put this data on the computer tonight.'

Steve Rocketto, a mathematician from Connecticut, wore faded US army denims. His dark glasses and forage cap had landed him two nicknames full of South American innuendo: '*El Piloto*' – he most certainly was, as he was soon due to get his local flying permit; '*El Bandido*' (bandit) – well, that quickly became the team joke. Steve was an astronomer at the Smithsonian Baker-Nunn Observatory based with the science faculty of the University of Arequipa, some 250 miles south-east of Nasca and 9,000 feet high in the clear air of the Andes. There he had made contact with Professor Lucio Salas of the university's engineering department, one of the best surveyors in Peru. With surveying assistants from the university and other members of the Smithsonian team, Gerald Hawkins had gathered a group of specialists whose research into the mysterious lines on the Nasca desert was to produce some surprising results.

In a twelve-month period from December 1967 Gerald Hawkins's team made six visits (a total of eighty-five man days) to Nasca. I joined them in July 1968 to film the climax of the survey when Hawkins himself arrived to work on the site. I had flown to Lima from the Caribbean shores of Colombia where I had been photographing wildlife with my wife Marion. On my first day in the Peruvian capital I met Hawkins for lunch at a long-established meeting place, the Gran Hotel Bolívar, and ensconced in leather-back chairs in the wood-panelled Colonial Bar, we had space to spread our maps and photographs of the Nasca plateaux.

My first impression was that somehow the astronomer had already solved the problem. He listened with sharp interest to my first-hand impressions of the site and Maria Reiche's views and asked some probing questions; but I suspected that my information was no more than supporting evidence for some notion he had already developed. If he had the solution, then what a scoop! So I asked for his opinion off the record.

No scientist likes to give an opinion, either on or off the record, without some basis, and it took him some moments to pick out one particular aerial photograph from the set supplied by the Peruvian Air Force.

'Well you see, Tony, it's all those lines pointing in those areas north and south – they're very puzzling.' I needed some explanation. All the lines seemed puzzling to me. Why single out the lines to the north and south? I felt a sense of helplessness at being out of my own field. Astronomy and wildlife seemed suddenly irretrievably disparate.

Many lines begin at centres, like spokes on a wheel hub.

'See here, these centres where the lines radiate or converge,' he continued.

I noticed dots on the print which I knew must have been stone piles and lines which radiated from other places, clearly isolated hills. Some of the lines he pointed to led from the edge of the plateau into the open desert, or to the large rectangular and trapezoidal features. I was impressed by his legal-cum-scientific precision of language: 'radiate *or* converge'. Yes, at this stage in the investigation, one could not be sure in which direction the lines were to be used.

'I'm suspicious of the calendar theory because most celestial activity occurs on the east and west horizons and we have to presume that the lines would point to risings or settings of the sun, moon and planets: stars would of course be visible on north and south horizons, but they rise in the same position night after night. They could hardly be calendric. I would really expect sun and moon lines, if this is to prove a calendar.' He saw my question coming and went on to explain.

'As the earth rotates on its axis once every twenty-four hours we get the impression that the sky is changing during the day and night. Other movements give us seasons, phases of the moon and so on. Most of the action is on the ecliptic, the zodiac. That part of the celestial sphere never gets to the north.'

I felt certain that Maria Reiche would have considered this point.

'Surely something must appear in the north and south? And if so, why not record the position with a line?'

Gerald Hawkins countered with a clear and precise argument.

'Of course a star will appear briefly for an hour or so over the north horizon, and then set, but few of those stars are important astronomically. There is the Big Dipper (Ursa Major) and Casseiopea, but those stars are second magnitude, not very bright. And in these latitudes, the Dipper is always upside down! Let us say that, astronomically speaking, the purpose of the lines is not immediately obvious.' Again, the scientist speaking – careful, unbiased, non-committal.

Over lunch I returned to the calendar theory. According to Maria Reiche and Paul Kosok the lines were designed to point to significant positions of heavenly bodies. The Nascas, being primarily agriculturalists, would have had a 'priesthood' of astronomers who used the alignments to predict the best planting seasons. Would they have needed a complicated calendar for that? If Gerald Hawkins's first assumption was correct, then what did the lines point to? Indeed, what was their purpose?

'That,' and he twisted the stem of his glass with a Holmesian air, 'is what I intend to find out.'

Having arranged to meet on the *pampa* the next day, I headed for a busy street behind the old San Marcos University to make a deal with a long-distance taxi driver. I would need the full five places in his car as space in which to spread out my camera gear. In return for offering me a good price, the driver would collect passengers in Nasca and continue south along the coast road to Arequipa. I could get another car for the return journey.

A fog covers Lima in July. In fact, although rain is almost unknown, the fog persists for nine months of the year, obscuring the sun and producing a strange gloom. Occasionally a particularly heavy *garua* or sea mist descends and leaves the streets glazed and slippery. It was in those conditions that I began my tenth journey to the Pampa de San José. Only six hours to go, I reckoned, and at an altitude of 1,500 feet I would rise above the worst of the coastal gloom and into the sunlight again. However, before starting the climb to the *pampa*, I stopped briefly at the Hacienda San Pablo for news of Maria Reiche. The caretaker of the small roadside house explained that the *Doctura* was away in Germany. He did not know when she would return. (She was working on her book, the second edition of *Mystery on the Desert*.)

By 1968 Maria Reiche had already published a few astronomical conclusions about the lines, but sadly the data has never been incorporated into a single volume. At that time, after twenty-three years on the Nasca desert, she reported that she had detected several apparently similar azimuths for lines which, she said, suggested that similar astronomical sightings had been made at widely separated figures or groups of lines. Perhaps the calendar was extremely complicated – something beyond the ingenuity of modern astronomy? Would the latest survey, backed up by thousands of computer calculations, prise the ultimate secret from the *pampa*? Could it prove the calendar theory? Was every line linked to a sky object?

I hurried on to Nasca where I found the survey team settled in the newly built Hotel Monte Carlo at the edge of the town. I was greeted by Hawkins.

'Hey, Tony, we've made progress. The computer result came through. The two mounds of the Great Rectangle aligned with the Pleiades between A.D. 600 and 700.' Then, as I looked puzzled, 'The

The Pleiades, the seven daughters of Atlas and Pleione in Greek mythology. This open cluster of several hundred stars in the zodiacal constellation Taurus was recognized by the people of ancient Peru. Six or seven of the stars can be seen with the unaided eye, and to the Indians of the coast they were known as *Fur*. The Incas said they were the *Qolqa* or 'Granary' and believed they watched over the preservation of seed.

An eastern extension of the Great Rectangle on the Pampa de San José aligns with the point where the Pleiades rose in 610 ± 30 years.

Pleiades – you know – the pretty little group of stars in Taurus the Bull. You can call it Plaza de las Pleiades if you want to.'

The exact date was confirmed, plus or minus thirty years, at A.D. 610 which almost matched the radiocarbon dating for a wooden post discovered in the early 1950s in a mound at the intersection of two lines on the Pampa de San José. Here was startling news at last, for if that kind of correlation between stars and lines could be found, there was certainly some basis for a calendar theory. Of all the stars, the Pleiades were probably the most significant to the ancient people of the Andes, and were recorded most frequently by various Spanish chroniclers. Known as Qolqa or 'granary', the Pleiades 'watched over the preservation of seed'.

Three and a half centuries ago Francisco de Avila, a Spanish priest with a doctoral degree from the University of San Marcos, produced a document concerning Indian star lore, in which he said that the Indians of the region of Huarochirí and San Damián – only a few miles east of Pachacámac – waited each year for the appearance of the Pleiades. If the stars rose large and bright, the crops would ripen well; if they were small, the people expected to suffer.

Pleiades then, all right – but what about the rest of the lines? Gerald Hawkins continued, 'Now for the bad news.' Not knowing what to expect, I said, 'How bad?' He chuckled at my concern. 'We can't see the stars! Well, anyway, not within two degrees of the horizon. There's so much haze, you can't even see the sun when it's setting. We expected clear skies.'

July was mid-winter and the coastal fog was affecting the observations of objects of second magnitude or less at horizon level, although, as I had predicted at our Lima meeting, the sky directly overhead was mostly clear blue.

'Anyhow,' continued Hawkins, who was apparently unperturbed by the conditions, 'we have almost completed a baseline, so we can check our ground position exactly against the photogrammetric survey the Peruvian Air Force will make.'

The next three days on the *pampa* were spent checking and rechecking the azimuths of some carefully selected lines and features, and determining our absolute geographical position at the baseline. Much of the work was in the hands of surveyors and '*El Piloto*' Rocketto, who had been to Nasca on three previous occasions for star photography as groundwork for the survey. The Peruvian team, being accustomed to the heat, had no problem staying on the *pampa* all day. The astronomers sweltered; as dust covered their skins, they looked more like Inca mummies as each day went by, or the dancers in the film *Zabriskie Point*.

Gerald Hawkins had figured out the details of the survey method in his office in Boston. To check the calendar theory he would need an accurate map of a large area. The photogrammetric survey would produce that. The method was simple yet scientifically rigorous. A precision camera would be carried in an aircraft flying over the desert with speed, height and course accurately controlled. Single pictures on wide film would be taken at intervals of about half a kilometre and these, when printed, would be laid together as a mosaic giving a highly accurate plan of the lines. A selected pair of photographs would be placed in a stereoprojector. Special optics would recreate the terrain. A tiny instrument would be made to move up and down over the image, as if it were crawling antlike over the actual surface, and a complete three-dimensional map would be made, accurate to one metre on the ground.

The final map was drawn on a non-stretch base. The scale was large: 1:2000. Ten centimetres on the plan equalled 200 metres on the ground and the contours were at metre intervals above sea level. All the desert markings that could be seen in the machine were drawn to scale: zigzags, radiating or starlike centres, and the parallel grids of lines. Apart from lines too narrow to show, and therefore omitted, every line was included: the limit of detail went down to lines about 10 inches wide. The final plans covered four large desktop-sized sheets and represented the area along the edge of the Ingenio valley, both east and west of the Pan-American Highway, and incorporating part of the Pampa de San José where the observation tower now stands. The baseline, laid down by Professor Salas, checked with the bearing obtained from the Peruvian National Grid, and so the correct aximuths for all the lines could be taken from the map and fed into a programmed computer.

I had been watching the elaborate care of the survey team as they toiled to get an accuracy of within a few seconds of arc demanded by the method – an accuracy which was of course potentially more precise than the original constructors could have obtained without instruments. Some of the most curious of all the lines described by Maria Reiche in her book were those aligned almost exactly north/south: she had said they were accurate to within less than one degree, and she had mentioned three specifically on the Pampa de San José, where the surveyors

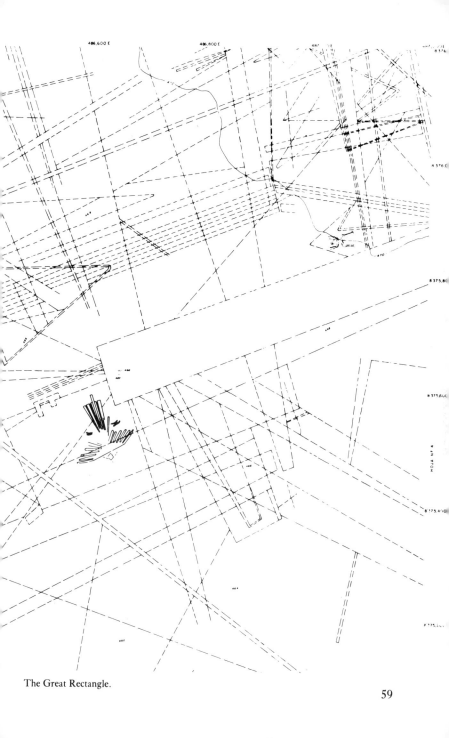

The Great Rectangle.

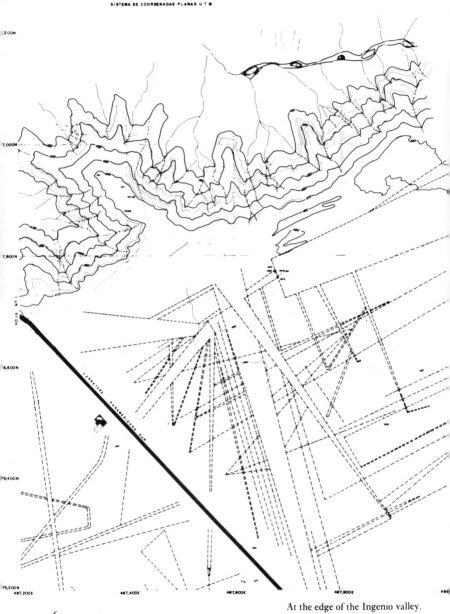

At the edge of the Ingenio valley.

Huarochirí is a typical Andean town.

and Gerald Hawkins were now at work. Maria Reiche also referred to more north/south lines on a tableland thirteen miles distant and used the large-scale parallelism as a pointer to some astronomical significance.

Gerald Hawkins was adamant. 'Finding north/south axis is a simple problem and it mustn't be used to imply sophisticated astronomy. A calendar or a radiating grid of lines where every line hits a star – now that would be very significant.'

Apparently to an observer watching a star rise over the north-eastern horizon and set on the north-western, a simple bisection of the angle gives north. Likewise the shadow of the sun falling from a post points south at noon in the southern hemisphere. True north is not of much use to primitive peoples. Nothing rises or sets there. Nothing happens astronomically. It is more like a fetish of a tidy mind, a 'surveyor complex'. The avenues of cities and state boundaries in the United States run north/south. Also the sides of the Giza pyramids.

If the north/south axis could be found in a simple way, surely here might be a reason for the duplication of other azimuths as reported by Maria Reiche? We knew that wooden posts once stood on the *pampa*. On any one day, all the shadows cast by those posts would point in the same direction and if on a feast day (established by a simple day count from the solstice or equinox and celebrated over a wide area) a line was constructed as an extension of the shadow, then large-scale parallelism would follow. Also when the shadow fell that way again, it would signal the next fiesta time. Maria Reiche had apparently spoken of lines marking the movement of the shadow of an important hill across the *pampa* on a solstice day.

Gerald Hawkins was still not to be moved.

'First of all you have to establish criteria,' he responded. 'Science demands proof, and speculation remains speculation until scientists as a whole accept the proof.'

Harsh words and even harsher standards to be met, as at Nasca there was little hope of turning that speculation into a proven theory from what was known of the Nasca people. They were no longer there and no written language was known, until it was brought in at the time of the conquest. The Spanish chroniclers are the only sources of ancient Andean star lore. In particular, Francisco de Avila and another Jesuit, Pablo de Arriaga, dealt at length with the ancient Andean religion.

They described what the Incas and other Indians told them at that time. They wrote often and in detail of the Pleiades. The Southern Cross – known as Chacana – was next in frequency; then Alpha and Beta Centauri called Llamapa Ñáwin – 'eyes of the llama' (the Andean humpless camel); the constellation Lyra, called Orquo-Cilyay, represented a particoloured llama and was worshipped by Andean shepherds; perhaps Cygnus too represented a llama; and certainly the Indians knew the particular dark spot in the Milky Way known to modern astronomers as the Coalsack. Francisco de Avila recorded that in Huarochirí one dark spot was called the Yutu or 'partridge'. In Inca lore the god of thunder drew water from the Heavenly River which the Milky Way represented. These would all be likely direction targets for the lines. The Pleiades had already shown up as a distinct possibility.

Venus, the brightest of the planets and recognized easily as the morning or evening star, featured strongly in some chronicles and, according to some interpretations, in a crude diagram of the Inca cosmos outlined by chronicler Juan de Santa Cruz Pachacuti. The morning star was prominent in Inca mythology, and called Chaska Qoylyor, or 'shaggy star'.

Although most of the records of the chroniclers concern the people of the highlands, where the air is crystal clear, the stars mentioned by them were of sufficient magnitude to be seen on the coast. One reliable source, Father Antonio de la Calancha, who was born in La Plata (now Sucre), the old capital of Bolivia, said that the Chimú people in northern Peru counted their year from the first appearance of the Pleiades over the eastern horizon.

What about the desert drawings and their possible astronomical correlation? Dr Paul Kosok, who had noticed a similarity between some desert drawings and certain designs on Nasca pottery, suggested that the drawings could be totemic, representing the original ancestor spirit of the individual clans or kinship groups of the Nasca people. He then related totem symbols to the constellations; the connection, he said, was not uncommon in some cultures elsewhere in the world at certain transitional stages of social development. Dr Kosok added, too, that old totem figures have sometimes become so identified with certain heavenly bodies or constellations that they have given their names to our constellations. Totemism, with clan names taken from wild animals, is typical of many forest tribes in South America, but was not the custom of the mountain Indian people.

Looking back to the chronicles again, Felipe Guamán Poma, writing in the early seventeenth century, said the Incas traced the 'shadows' or 'shapes' of men, women, plants and animals in the stars, though today not all historians would agree that his observations were reliable. From here the idea seems to have arisen that the figures represented the constellations venerated by the ancient Andean people.

When Gerald Hawkins decoded Stonehenge, Sir Fred Hoyle, the British astronomer, observed that it was the key architectural regularities of the massive stone circle and archways that fitted the theory. Here, at Nasca, there seemed a chance that if an animal figure fitted a constellation, and if a line that was part of the figure pointed directly to that constellation, then the astronomical interpretation could be taken as proven.

In 1952 an animal figure was discovered one mile south-west from the Great Rectangle that had now been found to align with Pleiades. It was a monkey, revealed as a beautifully drawn creature with a spiral for a tail (though twisting in the wrong direction to be anatomically equated with a prehensile tail). It is interesting on two counts. First, it is isolated from the main area of the lines and, second, Maria Reiche published a detailed astronomical interpretation of the figure in 1958.

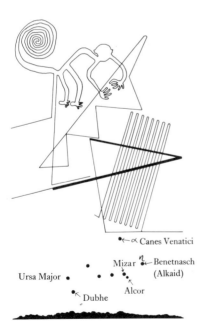

•←∝ Canes Venatici

Mizar *η* ←Benetnasch
(Alkaid)

Ursa Major •
Alcor

•←Dubhe

Ursa Major seen rising above the mountain-rimmed northern horizon at Nasca. In A.D. 1000 the star Benetnasch would have appeared above the end of the wide cleared area on the grid of sixteen lines. Though the constellation is well known in the northern hemisphere, and the Greeks saw the form of a bear outlined by the stars, it seems to have held little importance for ancient Peruvians.

Maria Reiche suggests that the figure which is generally regarded as a monkey represents the constellation Ursa Major, known to us as the Great Bear. She has calculated that the azimuth of the main cleared area she calls a *pista*, below the figure, suggests an orientation towards the rising and setting of a star known as Benetnasch at the tip of the 'tail' or 'handle' of the Great Bear constellation. The star is not visible in that position on the horizon in modern times and Maria Reiche suggests that it could have been seen 'around the year A.D. 1000'. Sixteen parallel lines cross the *pista* and she says they all have directions or orientations which pointed approximately to Benetnasch at that date.

I could see how she had reached that conclusion. She had worked from a standard Peruvian government map with a scale of 1 : 200,000, from which she calculated the latitude of the monkey site. Then, as she knew the azimuths of the sides of the *pista*, she was able to obtain a declination or the angular distance of a body north or south of the celestial equator on the celestial sphere. Maria Reiche found two declinations, one for each side of the *pista* and both within a fraction of a degree for the declination of 54.5 degrees at A.D. 1000, computed by Gerald Hawkins for the star Benetnasch.

So was the star theory still valid? As my aim was to double-check the available data, I asked Gerald Hawkins for a second opinion. We went to look at the figure on the ground. The monkey, measuring 260 feet from head to tail, was formed, like many of the other animal drawings, from a narrow twisting path that led across the desert and could be followed only by placing one foot in front of the other. Two simple piles of stones had been placed at the end of the *pista*. From my eye level of 5 feet 9½ inches there was no way of seeing the markings as being a monkey; the straight lines were more obvious and all the paths had been cleared in the same careful manner by removing the dark, stony desert pavement.

Yes, affirmed Hawkins, the *pista* did point in the direction of the rising of the star Benetnasch known on astronomical maps as Eta Ursa Majoris. 'But,' he said, 'there were other stars on these lines in the Nasca period.' Beta Casseiopea rose on the *pista* and set on the grid of sixteen lines in A.D. 1100. Alpha Casseiopea was so situated in A.D. 1600, Delta and Gamma Casseiopea in A.D. 900 and so were even more stars in the years before Christ.

The answer seemed clear: without a definite, narrow archaeological date, the lines could be made to fit any number of stars at different times. Maria Reiche's date of A.D. 1000 can be seen only as a purely arbitrary choice, unless it was backed up by dated archaeological finds from the site not recorded in her report.

How did the figure represent the Great Bear? In her 1958 astronomical interpretation, Maria Reiche suggests that the stars of the Great Bear – called by her Plecda, Megrez, Alith and Mizat – formed the two arms one above the other: the head would be represented by Alphae Canes Venatici. Dubhe, the brightest star in the constellation, was not included in the figure by Maria Reiche because she claimed it was so close to the horizon that it was invisible to the naked eye. Gerald Hawkins, however, says that in A.D. 1000 Dubhe (Alpha Ursa Major) was six degrees above the horizon even given a skyline altitude of three degrees allowed in the original report, so the pattern would somehow represent a monkey plus an extra star.

It would have helped if Maria Reiche had given a star map, because word descriptions are hard to follow. On the face of it there was some correspondence between the sky and the monkey except for the brightest star in Ursa Major. But it was not a good fit.

Yet Gerald Hawkins was willing to overlook the misfit up to a point and try to see the non-existent monkey. As he said, 'Even our own constellations don't exactly match the image. Casseiopea looks more like a "W" than a Queen, the legs of Taurus the Bull are not there, and Pegasus the Horse is really only a great square.'

What intrigued Hawkins was the spiral tail. Could it represent the endless revolution of the stars around the pole? This would be a remarkable conceptual connection for the Nascas, because the Pole Star was always below the horizon, invisible. They would have 'deduced' the circumpolar rotation by observing only the visible half-circles and segments.

Another desert figure reputedly aligned with the Great Bear is described in Maria Reiche's first Spanish edition of *Mystery on the Desert* as 'the famous cleared area on the road to Puquio'. The book is hard to find and I was lucky to get a copy from the British Council Library in Lima. The site was equally elusive. Like so many of the sites described in the book, we are not let into the secret of its exact location. There is however only one large drawing in that area – the same 'needle and ball of wool' I was shown by Josue Lancho. It comprises one long clearing with a zigzag passing through it sixteen times, leading to a spiral.

But could the main clearing have been aimed at the four stars of Ursa Major on the northern horizon? A wide clearing is hardly precise enough to claim a 'hit'. Marie Reiche suggests that it aligned with the

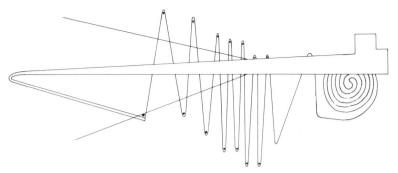

Stone piles mark the corners of the zigzag.

stars between A.D. 0 and A.D. 710. This time, however, instead of a monkey the drawing was a spiral and zigzag line, and though the number of bends in the zigzags are equal, the spirals turn in opposite directions. Also the date for alignment is between three and ten centuries different from the date she gave for the monkey of A.D. 1000. Hawkins thought the evidence too inconclusive to warrant a computer check.

When I left Nasca in July 1968, the survey team had completed the work that would eventually relate the *pampa* ground features to the map made by the Peruvian Air Force. Gerald Hawkins was to stay on for some days to photograph the extreme horizon, which in some directions was nearly 100 miles distant. Almost predictably the sky remained hazy and he was forced to give up and return to Boston. The photographs were not taken until December when Father Dungannon, a Jefferson City Mission priest working in Nasca, phoned Steve Rocketto in Arequipa and advised him of good visibility. '*El Piloto*' then flew a Piper Cherokee through the steep Andean foothills to Nasca to get the shots.

The final work of Gerald Hawkins's team was a careful traverse of two kilometres of the Pampa de San José along the line extending to the east of the Great Rectangle. That was made in the last days of 1968 just after Steve's flight through the foothills. The aim was to study the number of ancient Nasca ceramic vessels that lay in fragments, in the hope of dating them. Nasca pottery is divided into nine different phases, each conforming to a known time span of several decades. The most widely recognized classification was done by a team from the University of California, Berkeley. Gerald Hawkins was looking for a clue to the date or span of years during which the lines had been built.

67

N

Ingenio valley

Pan American Highway to Lima

Setting sun
June solstice
+24

"Grid of the Pleiades"

The Great Rectangle
"Plaza of the Pleiades"

Setting sun
December solstice
−24

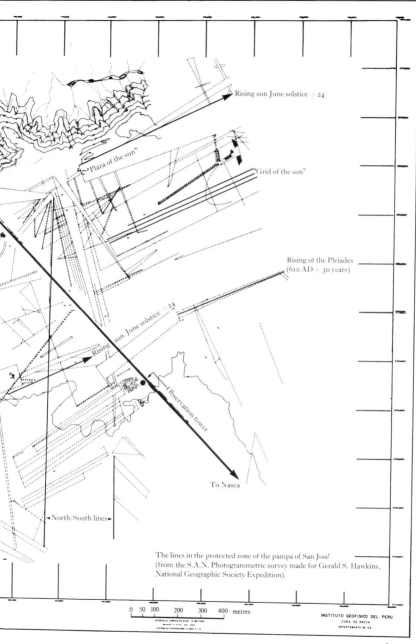

Rising sun June solstice + 24

"Plaza of the sun"

"Grid of the sun"

Rising of the Pleiades
(610 AD + 30 years)

Rising sun June solstice + 24

Observation tower

To Nasca

North/South lines

The lines in the protected zone of the pampa of San José
(from the S.A.N. Photogrammetric survey made for Gerald S. Hawkins,
National Geographic Society Expedition).

0 50 100 200 300 400 metres

INTERVALO CURVAS DE NIVEL 5 METROS

SISTEMA DE COORDENADAS PLANAS U T M

INSTITUTO GEOFISICO DEL PERU
ZONA DE NAZCA
DEPARTAMENTO DE ICA

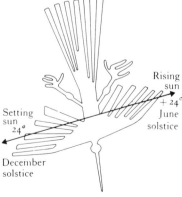

A line crossing the body of a large bird on the *pampa* to the south of the Great Rectangle aligns with the solstice positions of the sun setting in December and rising in June. But lines leading in other directions cross the tail of the bird.

Setting
sun
24°

December
solstice

Rising
sun
+ 24°
June
solstice

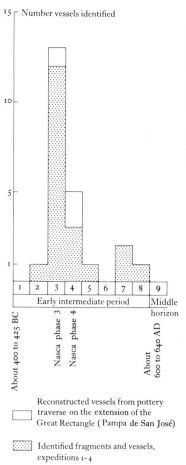

Number vessels identified

1	2	3	4	5	6	7	8	9

Early intermediate period | Middle horizon

About 400 to 425 BC

Nasca phase 3

Nasca phase 4

About 600 to 640 AD

Reconstructed vessels from pottery traverse on the extension of the Great Rectangle (Pampa de San José)

Identified fragments and vessels, expeditions 1-4

Nasca pottery sherds found on the Pampa de San José were examined by the expeditions of Gerald S. Hawkins. The pieces were identified and grouped in phases known particularly by the designs. It is the only quantitative evidence concerning the pottery artefacts on the Nasca *pampas*. Small numbers of fragments of later times were also found.

Diagram adapted from the Final Scientific Report for the *National Geographic Society Expedition, Gerald S. Hawkins.*

Just conceivably the pottery might have been placed on the desert before the lines were made, though most likely it was left there at the time of construction or after. Anyway, the possibility of a positive match-up between the date of the pottery and an alignment of several lines with star declinations for the same period could not be over-looked.

The team counted hundreds of fragments. When these were checked, the early intermediate period in Nasca prehistory was clearly domi-nant, though, in fact, the pottery represented the widest span from Nasca 2 (approximately 300 B.C.) to Late Nasca (A.D. 540). Numerically the Nasca 3 period, spanning two and a half centuries before the birth of Christ, was most abundant, as shown in the histogram, though of course the traverse only represented part of the Pampa de San José. This was the first suggestive evidence for the period of the great 'line-building'. However, careful archaeologists point out – logically – that we cannot be *sure* that the pottery and the lines are related.

In mid-1969 I was with Marion in the forests on the eastern side of the Andes. We were photographing a wildlife El Dorado on the River Manú, one of the Amazon headwaters. On our way over the Andes towards the coast, we had stopped in Nasca. Again there was no sign of Maria Reiche. The locals said she was there, but with so much desert about us there was little chance of encountering her. We pressed on to Lima. In the mail awaiting me there was a heavy envelope bearing the name of the Smithsonian Institution. At last, the long-awaited report by Gerald Hawkins – forty-four pages with an appendix of diagrams, photographs, maps and computer print-out. We rushed back to our hotel room to read it undisturbed.

The computer had been programmed to search for any sign that might indicate a special knowledge of astronomy, such as other early civilizations undoubtedly possessed. A fair presumption would be that if the Nascas built lines with considerable accuracy, and if those lines had been built to point to sun, moon, planet or a star position, the positions should include the important extremes in the case of sun and moon: each year the sun moves regularly to its summer and winter extremes, the solstices. Each month the moon does likewise. Some chronicles had confirmed that the Incas respected solstice and equinox dates although many historians doubt the reliability of those particular records.

Gerald Hawkins used the basic computer programme he had applied to Stonehenge, but with an adjustment for latitude. The machine printed out whether or not the sun or moon can be seen at the end of a line at one of the calendar extremes – midwinter setting, midsummer rising, etc. A special sub-routine was added for Nasca, and the machine searched for star correlations. The sun and moon change in their position of rising and setting day by day. The sunrise halts on the horizon when the declination is plus or minus $23\frac{1}{2}$ degrees. The exact declination depends on the tilt of the earth's axis (obliquity) – this was 24 degrees in 2000 B.C., slowly decreasing to $23\frac{1}{2}$ degrees today.

This daily position of the sun on the horizon on a particular calendar date does not change much over the centuries since the pattern is fixed by obliquity, the angle of tilt of the earth's axis. On the other hand, the moon when full turns at declinations which vary between 29 and 19 degrees. This complicated moon pattern, completing three cycles in fifty-six years, has been described in detail in Hawkins's *Stonehenge Decoded*.

As a first step, Gerald Hawkins measured in XY coordinates from the ground plan of three selected points on a line. He measured the centre axis of twenty-one thin triangles and of seventy-two of the straight line features including lines, parallel grids and edges of rectangles. What of the grids – the railway-track groups of lines? From each of these groups, only one line was put into the programme, otherwise the statistical result would have become biased. There were, on this basis, ninety-three measurable features on the plan, which Hawkins was certain were sufficient to test the theory. Each of the ninety-three had to be checked astronomically in both directions, since *a priori* one did not know which way they worked. To allow for errors on the part of the line builders, and any unavoidable small discrepancy that could have slipped into the measurements of the plans, the computer programme for Nasca was designed to tolerate and print out misalignments of up to one degree. These are normal expected errors in any measurement process. They are not to be confused with 'goofs'. Just occasionally our faith in computers is shattered by a thousand-fold increase in some punch-card household bill. The problem generally stems from inaccurate information punched into the card.

The print-out showed thirty-nine sun–moon alignments and some at least of these might truly be astronomical. This is more than twenty per cent. How many 'hits' would be expected by chance? The calendar extremes would be like targets on the horizon, a total of eighteen of them. Four solstice rises and sets for the sun, and a rise and set for the equinox, making a total of six sun targets. For the moon it is double – twelve. So, eighteen targets each two degrees wide (allowing for a maximum error of plus or minus one degree) gives a total target width of thirty-six degrees. This is one-tenth of the full 360-degree circle of the horizon, and so at least one in ten of the lines should point to the sun and moon *by chance* – that would be nineteen of the 186 fed into the computer. Gerald Hawkins discovered thirty-nine alignments with sun and moon, which was twenty above the number to be expected by chance. Certainly not all the lines could be thus explained. A few were good candidates for sun-calendar markers. But the entire maze was not a vast sun–moon–star calendar, as Paul Kosok had hoped.

Hawkins had confirmed that about twenty of the 186 possibilities might be thought of as calendric, though with some strong reservations. The lines pointing to the sun and moon were not unusually marked in any obvious way: apparently they were just ordinary lines, no different from the other eighty per cent which did not point to sun or moon. There was nothing to suggest that they were anything more than ordinary non-astronomical lines. The number of hits was close to 'random expectation'. Interestingly enough, though, the line through the condor was solsticial, and the condor could be argued to be a 'special' marker and the line therefore truly significant. Also the rectangle to the east of the area, marked by a long-beaked bird.

To check the alignments of stars and lines presented a problem which even now, at the time of writing, is only partly solved. The problem revolves around dating the lines. Precession means that lines would not point to the star positions as they are today and for every fifty years or so that the computer searched back into history, so a different star would appear as a target for a line. If a positive construction date had been available and if the lines were astronomical, then a large number of lines would have hit star targets near that date.

Without a known construction date the computer had to be programmed to search over a long time span. To take into account even the most extravagant claims for the age of the lines the computer was programmed to search from 5000 B.C. to the present day. This was despite the fact that the pottery traverse had indicated that the pots were of the first centuries B.C. and A.D. The lines could have come before the pots, or even vice versa. Whatever the age up to 5000 B.C., if the lines were aligned astronomically, the computer print-out would show it.

There was a distinct element of chance which could not be ignored. Spin a roulette wheel and the ball is certain to end on a number or zero. The computer print-out sheets were full of stars at the end of lines, so how to interpret the results? The machine had been fed the positions of the forty-four brightest stars, those brighter than magnitude $+2.0$, and the brightest star of the Pleiades, Eta Tauri, at magnitude $+2.9$.

With 186 line directions, and allowing for the slow drift of precession, we would expect about nineteen chance alignments with stars in any one century. The computer average was 17.3 star alignments per century, very close to theory. Some centuries were higher, some were lower. For centuries that matched the pots, the score was low – only seven stars from 100 B.C. and six from A.D. 0–100 (astronomers recognize

A.D. 0). Clearly there was no hope of arguing for a deliberate star-alignment grid for those centuries. Beyond the pottery time scale, between 3400 and 3300 B.C., thirty-one lines would have hit star targets, assuming of course that the lines were there at that time. Still this was only seventeen per cent of the lines under test – an unacceptably low percentage in terms of astronomy.

The computer had also checked for unidentified celestial objects which were visible when the lines were built and are not seen today. We know of them as novae, new stars, which shine brilliantly and then fade away: giant stellar explosions of immense volumes of incandescent gas that have attracted the eyes of men since they first watched the heavens. One such was in Taurus, which later formed the Crab nebula.

These brilliant bursts of energy last for a few weeks or months before fading to invisibility. Such transitory phenomena, sometimes suggested as the origin of the Star of Bethlehem, would surely have been noticed by Nasca astronomer priests, both on the Pampa de San José and elsewhere. If they had built lines to point to novae, then lines in widely different areas would hit the same target.

Gerald Hawkins compared lines near the valley edge at Nasca with those on the Pampa de San José fifteen miles away. He also made a second comparison with two well-shaped sites on the Pampa de San José. His results showed no significant overlap and his conclusion was that the line builders were not pointing to a set of celestial objects visible or recognizable. Were they pointing perhaps to U.F.O.s? I asked Hawkins. His reply was: 'First *you* prove that U.F.O.s exist!'

With the publication of the results of the 1968 survey I began to reconsider the lines mystery from a broader point of view. Gerald Hawkins had confirmed that the computer results would not support a time–clock–calendar theory and I concluded that even if some of the lines were built to the sun and moon, and one or two drawings, such as the monkey, pointed to the stars, most of the Nasca features were clearly non-astronomical.

To be sure, the survey and computer check had not eliminated solstice and equinox lines, and Maria Reiche emphatically said they existed – but there was now a scientifically proposed case for at least half of them being simply chance alignments. If not at the stars, sun and moon, then what did the vast majority of the lines point to? The answer to that question had to lie beyond the computer and certainly beyond Nasca whose peoples had been destroyed by a series of wars, epidemics and conquests until the valley was virtually depopulated.

4 More Lines

Eight and a half years had passed and it was 1977 before I could return to the mystery of the desert lines. In the intervening years I had travelled extensively through much of South America with Marion until, after an accident on an Andean road, a long spell in hospital gave me time to reconsider Nasca from a broader view. At that time I made up my mind that I would examine other lines and look for peoples in the Andes who had retained cultural links with the past.

Duncan Masson, the retired Scottish engineer, had suggested I look at more lines at a place twenty-five miles north of the Pampa de San José where, after leaving the Pan-American Highway and following a rough track, I found a broad, slightly sloping *mesa*. The map gave it as the Pampa de Media Luna. A fitting name perhaps. Pampa of the Half Moon. Why?

The Pampa de Media Luna is only twelve miles from the Pampa de San José, but the surface is sandy and all the lines were made by gathering small stones into heaps, or arranging stones in rows.

Following Duncan's precise directions I soon found his recommended camping place behind a low spur of the mountains and I laid out my sleeping bag beside the Volkswagen. My provisions were equally uncomplicated: packet soup and bread from Nasca. My petrol pressure-stove took only a couple of minutes to set up.

After supper, I walked across the desert: the moon was almost full, suspended just above the horizon, its usual brilliant silvery light dulled by haze into pale orange-brown. Yet there was no doubt in my mind that the Nascas would have been impressed. The Southern Cross was just visible towards the south-east. Although Gerald Hawkins's results had clearly discouraged a connection between the lines and astronomy on a one-to-one basis, I had a lingering suspicion, not supported by the computer, but still there for some deeper reason. Certainly Maria Reiche was as firmly convinced as ever.

Alone and without torchlight, stepping slowly across an otherwise empty desert, I felt the immensity of space. Not a sound, no muted animal cry, just sand, the moon and the splendour of the night sky. Could the line builders have seen to work in the dark? How would they have marked the sighting points? With lights perhaps? Yet no trace of lamps had been discovered. After several minutes, I picked out the shadowy outline of an electricity cable pylon against the sky: the wires must have led to an iron mine at Marcona, in the desert south of Nasca. Near one of the pylons the yellow track marks of a caterpillar construction vehicle stood out sharply in contrast to the dark sand, silently emphasizing that when the Nasca lines were built they must have 'shone' in much the same way on brightly moonlit nights. But on the other hand I could not see far and some Nasca lines are more than five miles long. Also, I asked myself, why so straight – over hills and gullies without apparent deviation – and stretching out beyond the horizon? I walked slowly back to the car, pondering these problems.

As I pulled the sleeping bag around my head, a shooting star left a fine trail across the southern sky. How would ancient men have responded to such mysteries? The Spanish priests had never described any sophisticated knowledge of astronomy of the type Gerald Hawkins had been persuaded to search for; the star-lore of the Andes was apparently mostly mythology about which I would need to know more. That shooting star, perhaps no more than a pea-sized pellet of iron or stone, a fragment of a planet or comet, had begun its journey in space – a dimension now visited by man and at least partly understood. On what grounds could I apply modern concepts of astronomy to lines made hundreds, perhaps thousands, of years ago?

The next morning the horizon and sky overhead were lost in a heavy grey mist – not dust pollution but fog. Although the high Nasca region, being well inland, is usually reckoned to be above coastal fog, there are times when it is affected by the foggy conditions created by the cold Peruvian or Humboldt current, fed from the bottom of a deep trench close to the shore. In some years the conditions are exacerbated by a periodic phenomenon locally named the *niño*, or 'child'. The name has grown from the tendency of the *niño* to occur near Christmas, when an insurgence of a warm water current from the north causes heavy rain showers over the desert coastline. When the winter fogs are exceptionally heavy some of the normally barren land is covered with a fine growth of flowering plants.

Computers cannot walk across a desert and search for clues – and that was my first objective that morning. I retraced my footsteps of the previous evening across the sandy wasteland. It was different from the San José *pampa*: mostly a coarse grey-brown sand covered the familiar yellow dust. My footprints led along a sharply curving route into the distance, and I would challenge anyone to walk a perfectly straight line in the dark.

Whatever it was, I had passed it in an instant. Peripheral vision is one of man's more useful abilities and the 'corner of my eye' had registered a line at right angles to my path. I had missed it in the night and as good as missed it in broad daylight. Without turning, I stepped back two paces, then half a step more and the line clicked into focus. There it was. A straight line, perhaps a mile long. At one end was a large hill, and at the other I could just see a low mound. This line was different. Instead of the cleared desert pavement that made the San José lines resemble shallow troughs, the line on Half Moon Pampa had been built of small heaps of stones, set approximately two yards apart, with a smooth path running to one side where even the smallest fragments of stone had been cleared. I followed the line in both directions and found that larger stone heaps had been built at each end of the line: one at the foot of the hill, and the other in the central expanse of the *pampa*. Here I stumbled upon two small fragments of ceramic which could be identified as Nascaware, though there were not sufficient sherds to recognize the original shape of the vessel.

From the hill at the eastern end of the line I checked the azimuth – approximately 240 degrees – and probably of no astronomical significance. Then I noticed that the line, although apparently straight from end to end, had almost imperceptible breaks along its length. Maria Reiche, I remembered, had noticed the same feature on the Nasca desert. The line might have been constructed in stages – perhaps the breaks marked the length of a measuring cord?

Hills, stone piles and pottery fragments were clearly becoming common factors. The pottery had probably been placed there with a purpose, and either smashed at that time or sometime afterwards. Gerald Hawkins had succeeded in reconstructing one round-bottomed vase from pieces found on one spot. He had also found the remains of five vessels right at the top of a 1,000-foot-high hill on the east side of the Pampa de San José. At the time he asked: 'Why did the Nascas carry the pots up the hill? Surely, unlike Everest, it wasn't climbed just because it was there.' Although the hill was difficult to climb, people had left traces of ceremonies and culture at its highest point and Gerald Hawkins had concluded that 'the mountain must have had a meaning to them'.

'The desert in all directions was equally rich – fragments scattered on the surface, on the mounds and between the black glazed stones.'
Gerald S. Hawkins, *Beyond Stonehenge*.

This pot was reconstructed and photographed on the Pampa de San José. It has been identified as Nasca 3 or 4 – about 2,000 years old.

That meaning had been noted independently by a priest four centuries earlier when, sometime between 1570 and 1574, Jesuit José de Acosta visited Nasca. Indians there had pointed to a great mound of sand, which they said was the chief shrine of the ancients. The chronicler left no doubts that high places had a special meaning for the ancient Peruvians, and even today the mountain Indians respect hills as sacred, spirit places.

Later that same day I found more lines on the Pampa of the Half Moon together with large rectangles and avenues with edges delineated by rows of stones. The method of construction had been dictated by the available materials and the surface, otherwise the features were essentially similar to those on the Pampa de San José. Knowing I would find more lines, I moved on north to Ica.

As I turned into the driveway of Duncan Masson's home, I was deeply preoccupied by two questions: if the purpose of the lines was not astronomical, what was it? And the fogs – were they becoming thicker? Was the atmosphere clearer in the past? As a long-time resident of the desert area, Duncan Masson would know about the weather. I needed to have more information before I could accept Gerald Hawkins's view that horizon sighting of the stars of second magnitude was impossible for much of the year. An alternative suggestion had been made by Maria Reiche at her London lecture when she said that pollution (particularly from the iron mine opened in 1959–60) was adversely affecting the climate.

The tyres of the Volkswagen crunched on gravel and Duncan's dog, a German shepherd, bounded from behind the house, followed at a more leisurely pace by its owner.

'How did you get on?'

'Fine,' I responded, '*no hay problemas*' – the local way of saying everything went well. 'The camp site was as you left it and the moonlight – splendid.'

Duncan laughed.

'But I've a pile of questions needing answers,' I continued.

'That's what I'm here for,' Duncan said and he stood back as if ready for an interrogation. 'I've been over so much of this desert and never written a word about it. I only write letters to the papers!' He laughed again. 'And sometimes they print them.'

After four hours together studying the maps, during which Duncan's Peruvian wife, Marta, provided us with lunch, we set out again for the desert. I was to be shown two new sites. Neither had been recorded before, although both were known to the foremost archaeologists in Peru and the United States. One site was particularly interesting as it was located beside an early settlement that had been accurately dated.

Our route lay along the western side of the Ica valley, and after

A line on the Peña de Tajahuana.

The Peña de Tajahuana near Ica.

following a sandy farm track for half an hour we arrived at a weathered rocky spur jutting into rich green fields of cotton. The contrast between fertile valley and desert was as sharp as at Nasca, and beneath the barren shoulder a cluster of trees had been offering shade for centuries.

'Pull in under those *huarangos*.' Duncan pointed to an isolated group with low branches, forming a natural awning. He saw my curiosity, and explained, 'The cows have shaped them that way, sheltering there to keep out of the sun.'

We locked the car and began to climb the hill, following a meandering track which Duncan reckoned had been made by the *huaqueros* many years ago.

'They call this hill the Peña de Tajahuana. Locally *peña* means rock or crag; said another way, it can mean hard work.'

After about fifty feet of steep ascent we had a good view down to the valley and to the expanse of desert ahead. Two low and rounded hills lay beyond us on a gently rising slope, while beyond them a backdrop of magnificent sand dunes with finely sculpted ridges stood like a wall perhaps 300 feet high.

We reached an earlier rampart that followed the contours of the hill. A second rampart had been built behind the first, and the outlines of two more showed clearly. These must have been ancient defences, used by early hill settlers. On every side lay opened graves: not of fallen warriors, as I first suggested, but of the people themselves, the early farmers of the Ica valley. An expedition from the University of California had visited the site in the 1950s and dated the fortified site at roughly 600 B.C.

The disturbed ground was littered with the debris hurriedly thrown out of the graves by treasure-hunters looting ceramics and weavings, probably worth a fortune on the black market. Among the pieces apparently considered worthless by the *huaqueros* were fragments of shells, some bivalve molluscs, perhaps from the Ica river, or more likely

Fragmented shells scattered among debris from graves on the Peña site – (above).

Peña de Tajahuana. Above: a simple path leads to a cairn of stones on a hilltop. Right: at the southern end of the site a wide clearing was made between a hill and the edge of the open ground.

from the sea. Remembering that shells had been found on the Nasca *pampa*, I examined these carefully. The material was crumbly, and must have been exposed to the desert climate for a long time, but sufficient remained to determine that they were not the well-known spondylus, a thorny oyster, as Duncan informed me, which came from the northern waters near the equator and was traded commercially. These shells might well have been of an edible shellfish and been buried as necessary food for the dead, or they could have been offerings.

'There's one of the lines.' Duncan pointed to the nearest hill, now a little over a hundred yards away. A line showed clearly where the stony surface had been cleared, leaving a path approximately two feet wide heading from the base of the hill directly to the summit.

The scramble to the top had left us breathless but we were rewarded by the sight of more lines leading to our hill, one from an open plateau to the north-west and another from a low hillock, out of sight when we had begun to climb. We spent another two hours tracing the lines and we located two large cleared areas, one a rectangle and the other a trapezoid seventy-nine feet across at the widest point. Near the end of

the rectangle I stopped to photograph small heaps of stones set out in neat rows: it was the same feature I had seen at Nasca. I also found pieces of broken ceramic, thin delicately coloured Nascaware of the third or fourth phases – the same age as the sherds found by Gerald Hawkins on the Pampa de San José. Duncan suggested the heaps had been made as the area was cleared. Like Josue Lancho, he looked for a simple answer.

'Even today, you see people making stone piles like these in the fields,' he said. I remembered how such piles of gathered stones were common in cultivated parts of the stony *altiplano* or Andean high plain near Lake Titicaca. In every respect the lines on the Peña de Tajahuana were comparable to those on the Pampa de San José and on the Pampa de Media Luna. Very obviously most of them were perfectly straight pathways connecting hills.

Duncan took me to another site on a flat sandy part of the desert. There he showed me piles of rounded stones: they were not glacial erratics but must have been carried from the mountains five miles away. When he discovered them in the 1950s, he had found an unbroken dull brown pottery dish upturned on the ground near a low stone heap. The strong afternoon winds had scoured the sand away. Underneath the dish he found a narrow-necked vase of the Ica Period (sometime between A.D. 900 and A.D. 1400).

'Empty?' I asked.

'Yes, nothing but a trickle of sand inside,' he replied.

How many more extraordinary places did this explorer know about? Had I seen the large trapezoid on the desert beside the Pisco valley, one river to the north of Ica? There seemed to be some connection between that and some perfectly straight paths or lines in the valley, and he referred me to a report and produced a map made by the University of Florida. He had discovered a huge trapezoid 2,132 feet long (only 750 feet shorter than the Great Rectangle on the Pampa de San José), 213 feet wide and ninety-two feet wide at the narrower end. Even more remarkable, he had also found a row of buried wooden stakes. He estimated there were over 300 of them, set in a line down the trapezoid's centre, to the half-way mark. Above ground they had either rotted or been snapped off and had disappeared.

When I asked if the line of the stakes had been perfectly straight, Duncan said no, he felt there were clear breaks in the alignment. And for what reason did the ancient people of the desert erect three hundred posts within a huge trapezoidal clearing? Duncan shrugged.

'It was totally different to the Estaquería at Nasca,' he said, reminding me of the site at the edge of the Nasca valley where rows of *huarango* posts stood in a huge Nasca cemetery. The purpose of the Estaquería posts is unknown, though possibly they supported a roof. I had checked the alignment of the Estaquería posts – an azimuth of 260 degrees. Duncan's trapezoid had one side at 260 degrees and the other at 252 degrees. The two sites were 100 miles apart and that azimuth, too, was similar to the line I had first seen on the hills at the southern end of the Ica valley, near Ocucaje. Was this a coincidence? If not, how could the similar azimuths be accounted for?

Duncan pointed to the west. 'On the way to the sea across the Tablazo de Ica,' he said, 'I found a small hillock, man-made I should think.' And he went on to describe in some detail another site featuring a wooden post. The remains of the post stood on the hilltop in the ground and Dr Jorge Muelle, an eminent Peruvian archaeologist, believed it was an *intihuatana* or sun post. Few *intihuatanas* survived the Spanish attempts to eradicate the old Andean religion, but tradition suggests that they marked places where the sun was worshipped: perhaps too, they were used as sundials.

Returning to my preoccupation with the lines at Nasca, I put another

A base of a wooden post (one of over 300 in a trapezoidal clearing) was discovered in the Ica desert in the 1950s. The dry climate had preserved every detail, including the bark. A sample taken from a similar post found on the Pampa de San José was radiocarbon-dated at between A.D. 445 and A.D. 605.

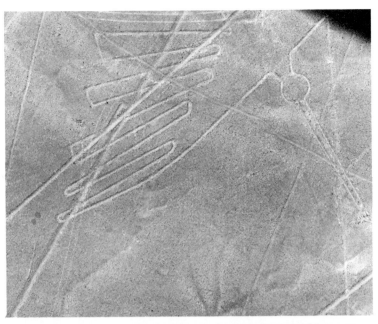

Are the animal figures and lines connected? Mostly the lines cross the designs without clear connections. In the case of the bird (top left), the picture (bottom left) and the 'whale' (above), the lines appear to have been made after the figures.

question. Had the lines, cleared areas and animal drawings been used at the same time? Were they of the same age? Duncan replied that he had studied some of these problems on the Pampa de San José; he had even attempted to measure the depths of lines where they crossed figures, hoping to establish a 'stratigraphy'. In some instances, such as where the prolonged beak of the humming bird terminates in a line, he concluded that the line and drawing seemed to have been made at the same time. In other cases where the line-junctions had been disturbed, he could not be so sure. More frequently the straight lines clearly had been constructed over the drawings with apparent disregard for the continuity of the twisting paths.

Drawings have been so disturbed all over the Nasca *pampa* that they often seem to be extensions of the lines. Aerial photography, however, reveals otherwise. When I photographed the desert markings from the air with false colour infra-red film and strongly filtered black and white, Duncan Masson's suspicions were upheld that many of the figures were beneath the long lines.

As a naturalist the animals on the Nasca *pampa* had always held a special interest for me, as many of the types, allowing for artistic interpretation, can be seen today in the nearby valleys, rivers and sea. Humming birds, condors, foxes, lizards and fish would have been part of the everyday life of the Nascas. It is true that there are no monkeys in the Nasca valley today but they still occur on Peru's north coast and in western Ecuador. It seems likely that there would have been trading contact with people from both these regions, and it has also been suggested that the Nascas could have maintained links with the Amazon forest tribes, only 220 miles distant across the Andes in a straight line. Whatever the origin of monkeys at Nasca, their remains have been found in graves of their hominid owners. The Mochica people of the same Pacific coast only 600 miles north and roughly of the same dates as the Nascas, kept monkeys as pets, and Larco Hoyle, a respected private collector and archaeologist, reported that designs in the form of a monkey were known on Mochica pottery. At Paracas, only 125 miles from Nasca, monkey skins were found in a grave.

Of the two monkeys most likely to be represented on the Pampa de San José the capuchin, with its grey-brown crown of hair resembling a monk's cowl, is still found in north Peru. Capuchins make the traditional pets kept by street traders. Also capuchins have noticeably protruding ears, a striking feature of the Nasca *pampa* drawing. Spider monkeys found in western Ecuador are not commonly kept as pets. They do possess gangly arms and legs like the Nasca beast but do not have protruding ears.

At her lecture in London in 1976, Maria Reiche suggested the spider drawing might represent the constellation Orion. The three stars of Orion's Belt were known to the Spanish as the 'Tres Marias' – The Three Marys – and according to Father Calancha, writing in 1638, those stars were well known to the Chimú people of the Jequetepeque valley in northern Peru. So, some connection between the Nasca pampa spider and Orion might be possible. It was not checked by Hawkins, because the line was too narrow to show on the air survey. A rough estimate from photographs shows that it does go 'somewhere near' Orion.

Duncan Masson reminded me of the mythology concerning spiders on the coast. 'They were used for divination a long time ago,' he said, 'and you know we've got the poisonous black widow spiders here too. We find them in the ditches and around the house.' It seemed to us that one explanation for the Nascas' reverence for spiders could lie in

Towards Orion.

This drawing of a spider on the Pampa de San José is over 140 feet long and close to the northern edge of the Great Rectangle. The line crossing the figure points in the direction of Orion the Hunter. Maria Reiche has suggested it might have been a deliberate alignment.

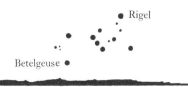

The constellation Orion rising above the Andes. Adapted from *Splendor in the Sky*, Gerald S. Hawkins.

their poisonous strength. Another spider of the coastal region belonging to the family Loxocelidae, or brown spiders, is also poisonous.

One seventeenth-century document in the *Legajos de Idolatría* (literally – 'the Files on Idolatry') in the Archbishopric of Lima mentions spiders used for divination. Apparently *echizeros* or sorcerers took a hollow bone, and after plugging one end with mud, inserted black spiders and then sealed the other opening. When the plugs were broken and the spiders fell on the ground 'the way they fell and the number of legs were important signs'.

Of the other animals represented in the desert drawings the condor has a special place in present-day Indian folk-lore and the fox might have represented an important god: Father Calancha wrote of an idol in the form of a Golden Fox at Pachacámac. It is possible that the outline of certain revered animals was seen in the stars and then portrayed on the ground, although it might be equally convincingly argued that the figures were created in homage to other ancient gods.

Gerald Hawkins had no opinion about the relation of lines to figures, except that a theory that 'lines-passing-through-figures are astronomical' cannot be supported unequivocally. Neither had he reached any conclusion about the age of the lines. Maria Reiche, on the other hand, believed that lines had been added to the Nasca complex over an unknown period of several centuries due to adjustments made by the astronomer priests as they compensated for precession drift. I concluded that the long lines were probably later than the figures or certainly must have held some special priority as their courses frequently disregard the figures' fine artistry. The lines too often were uncompromising: they led straight over the figures.

Spirals and animals are characteristic designs of the early phases of Nasca style pottery. While more than a hundred spiral patterns have been found on the surface of the Nasca *pampas*, few of the animal designs on the ground bear a strict resemblance to the painted pottery. The exception is the so-called 'killer whale' (top) – Nasca Phase 2 (approximately 300 B.C.).

The evidence for a purely astronomical use of the lines looked slim. Moreover there was Gerald Hawkins's observation that the haze above the horizon at Nasca obscured the stars, and it seems possible that this haze could have been heavier a thousand or more years ago, as some evidence suggests that the *loma* or fog vegetation on the desert coast was thicker then. Maria Reiche points out that the sky had been clear in Nasca in the 1940s and she believes that the climate is changing now with pollution affecting the weather.

I feel that the current changes are no more than the effect of the periodic changes in the cold Peruvian current. I had asked Duncan Masson about the weather. He confirmed Maria Reiche's comment that there had been three years of heavy mist and occasional heavy rain (the last *niño* was in 1972–73), and even in normal years the winter mornings were misty. For a few days each year the fog persisted for the full twenty-four hours.

Another factor to emerge was that the labour involved in clearing the *pampa* to make the lines had not been enormous. Gerald Hawkins had timed his team clearing a small area and, on the basis of Maria Reiche's estimate that the cleared area of all the lines totalled a square mile, Hawkins estimated they were no more than three weeks' work for 1,000 ancient Nascas. (For the BBC film made later in the year, Señor Lancho's class of schoolboys took twenty-five minutes to build a straight line of $171\frac{1}{2}$ yards long and twenty-four inches wide.)

I decided to ignore for the moment the large cleared areas – the so-called 'landing strips' or ceremonial gathering places – as well as the animal figures and spirals. I would concentrate on the pattern of lines that remained, including those radiating like spokes from several distinct hub-like centres. These centres are marked by hills or piles of stones, both sacred to the ancient people of the Andes. My hunch was that the radiating lines were by far the most important of all the markings, much as Maria Reiche had suggested in Nasca, although my reasons were different.

My first hypothesis was that the centres or stone piles were observation points used by astronomer priests in 'surveying' paths (or lines) to a star, sun or moon. This would require confirmation of their astronomical basis and Gerald Hawkins's work did not find any overwhelmingly positive astronomical correlation. The lines could have been visible on moonlit nights, but then the sky would be too bright to observe many stars, and anyway it is likely that the horizon was often obscured.

A line in the Atacama desert 500 miles from Nasca. The stone walls near the line are of fairly recent times, but the site is best known for its numerous worked-stone tools and arrow heads.

There was another obvious alternative: to look at the problem the other way round. Instead of an observer sitting on the pile of rocks watching for heavenly phenomena, perhaps the stones or hills themselves were the foci and the lines converged on these points – rather than radiating from them? On checking the published data and looking at the hundreds of pictures I had of the Nasca site, I did not doubt that the lines connected one centre to another, often a site in the valley to another on the *pampa*. A small number simply ended in the desert, at deliberate piles of stones which were not simply the rubble left by line builders.

So, if the lines were some form of pathway, probably religious, why were they so straight? The sheer precision of the lines indicated some special importance – an accuracy of four yards in a mile even over rough uneven ground. Why? And which were the more important: the paths or the heaps of stones, the hills and other centres? A desire to maintain the straightness in the lines must have been common to many people over a wide area of the central Andes as I knew of many other lines equally as straight as those in Nasca. They were, in fact, very numerous. Paul Kosok had mentioned other sites south of Nasca towards the Chile border and noted that cleared areas existed in the north of Peru in Zaña and Lambayeque, in the Virú valley and near Lima in the Lurín valley above Pachacámac. Gerald Hawkins also estimated that as many as 100 such sites existed in the coastal region, and I had heard of sites in the Atacama desert of Chile and had personal experience of others high in the Andes.

I decided to study photographs of as many of these as possible. After leaving Ica, my first call was to the headquarters of the Peruvian Air Force Photographic Service (S.A.N.) in a quiet tree-lined suburb of Lima, called Barranco. Archaeologists, road builders and planners, students – all are welcome to use the extraordinary facilities of S.A.N. Rows of filing cabinets are crammed with complete sets of aerial photographs of Peru; some pictures taken from directly above the ground, others oblique, showing the subject in a setting of a distant background. I saw stone forts set on mountain ridges, mud pyramids standing squarely in the coastal valleys, sturdy defensive walls, ancient canals, long irrigation ditches unchanged in 1,500 years, and oil pipelines – a large-scale visual history of Peru. Alferez Alcedo, the Peruvian Air Force officer who showed me round, pointed to a wall where blown-up photographs of the Nasca lines were displayed. He explained how in the 1940s S.A.N. had helped Paul Kosok, and later Maria

A pile of boulders at the end of a Collique path.

Reiche – and more recently, as I knew, produced the Nasca map for Gerald Hawkins.

My quest was for other lines. The first area that attracted me was Collique or Cantogrande, close to the capital, where a rapidly growing suburb is now destroying some ancient markings. I had been shown some pictures of this area in 1968 by Ted Pelikan, a long-time Lima resident and a resourceful weekend explorer. He had visited a place where ancient roadways and markings, similar to those at Nasca, led from a level valley bottom into the precipitous defiles or *quebradas* at the foot of the Andes. Ted Pelikan had noticed centres from which lines radiated: he had found himself at a hub of five or six radiating clearings or stone spokes, each varying, as he said, 'from five to eleven paces across'. The stones had been cleared and placed at the edges, yet he felt they were not highways – the practical correlations of transportation had not been their prime concern.

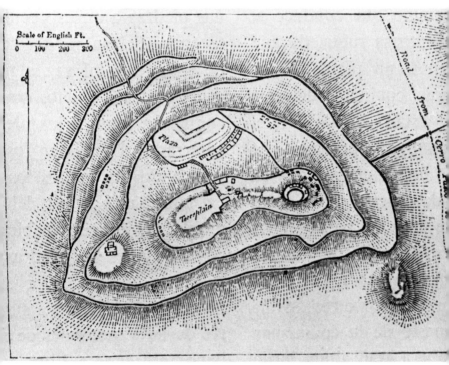

A fortified hill at Collique was mapped by the American Ephraim Squier over a hundred years ago.

Alferez Alcedo knew of the area and quickly produced the square 7 × 7 inch photogrammetric photographic print. With a viewer based on the principles of the Victorian stereoscope, I examined a pair of photos. At first I saw nothing but flat desert. I moved the shots a fraction of an inch and, as my eyes adjusted, the valley suddenly became a living place. Admittedly, the hillsides appeared larger than life, as the system exaggerates the vertical plane, but the distortion was useful as the raised edges of the lines, otherwise very low features, were emphasized. The lenses do not distort the horizontal plane and straight lines remain straight. I laid a ruler against one, nearly three miles long, and found no deviation in its direction. This was the first of many visits to S.A.N. and I succeeded in locating many of the lines that had been described. I found that none in Peru was as extensive as at Nasca and often they had been partly covered by windblown sand. Straightness of a line between places often miles apart was common to all the sites.

The Collique lines near Lima had long been known – exactly how long I was unable to confirm. Ephraim George Squier, a renowned American traveller who arrived in Peru on a diplomatic mission in 1863, had visited the valley: he made a drawing of a small fortified hill which was published in his book. But it seems that he did not see the lines. Other more recent writers, however, including Dr Hans Horkheimer, have recognized Nasca features in the Collique valley and I was given the most up-to-date information by María Rostworowski de Diez Canseco, director of the National Museum of History in Lima.

Speaking in perfect English – she had been to school in England – María Rostworowski led me through the museum, once the house of General San Martín, and immediately after him, Simón Bolívar, two of colonial South America's most famous independence fighters. A wooden verandah at one side of a central patio now overlooked a garden filled with trees and scented tropical flowers.

María Rostworowski was positive in her advice.

'Try to look at the problem from the Andean point of view. Delve into the Andean mind,' she said. She was reiterating what Gerald Hawkins had meant when he said: 'Look beyond the computer – the answer is beyond mathematics.' With something approaching sixteen years' experience in the Andes, I felt I had a good foundation and I listened intently. What I should need to do, María Rostworowski felt sure, was to study and understand the customs and religion of the people through the chronicles. Information about lines existed in the chronicles and much was known already especially to ethnohistorians – those people

An Aymara Indian sells coca leaves picked from bushes grown on Andean slopes. The leaves are dried before they are pressed tightly into bales to be carried over the mountains on mules or trucks.

who studied the customs of the people through the records in old documents.

'Lima,' María Rostworowski explained, 'is one of the great repositories of colonial history. Here we have the records of the Spanish clergy who observed the old religion first hand.'

And of those lines in Collique?

'Well known,' she said and mentioned that some years ago a local university research group had made an exciting discovery there. Apparently Peruvian experts made six visits to the site and an American anthropologist, Patricia Netherly, had taken photographs. What did they find? The stone-lined avenues as Ted Pelikan had shown me, and a small standing stone in a stone circle, and something more. They moved one of the larger stones and beneath it found a handful of flat leaves, greyish-brown and brittle – each about the size of a thumbnail which they identified as leaves of a coca plant.

Erythroxylon coca is the botanical name of a small bush, native to the Andes, and cultivated extensively by the Andean people for its leaves, which contain a small percentage of the drug cocaine. These days cocaine is commonly used in synthesized forms in modern surgery and illegally as a narcotic. In pre-Columbian South America the coca leaf was respected by the native people and the tradition of respect has continued to the present day among many Andean Indians. They chew the leaves with an alkaline earthy material (usually made from the ash of certain plants, bones or sea shells), and minute quantities of cocaine produce not a 'high' but a slight dulling of the senses to alleviate feelings of hunger, thirst and weariness. To turn the leaves into concentrated pure cocaine requires some knowledge of chemistry, and the native Andeans have never reached such a level of sophistication. In Inca times, coca leaves were highly respected and available only to the nobility, or as offerings. In the early colonial days, the Spanish introduced coca to all classes of Indian society and the well-organized coca plantations were enlarged. Most Andean Indians today still treat the use of the leaf with simple ceremony. They slowly and deliberately select the best leaves from their coca pouches or *chuspas*, discussing the quality of the coca in much the same way as cigar smokers talk of their favourite brands. They examine each leaf for imperfections, turning it in their fingers before they chew and savour it – as a wad like a quid of tobacco.

Aware of the mysterious power of the drug, the Indians made offerings of the leaves to their gods and spirit places. The coca leaves beneath the stone at Collique must have been an offering to a spirit that at one time was thought to reside there. María Rostworowski referred me to a seventeenth-century dictionary of the Indian language. Listed under 'coca' was *coca phahuatha* or the coca that 'was poured over the *guacas*'. (This last word was also written, phonetically, as *wak'as*, and in

Spanish as *uacas* and later as *huacas*.) The chronicles, she said, referred to many forms of *wak'as*: stones, hills, springs, caves and other inanimate objects, even sometimes the mummies of ancestors. All were revered. Many seemed to be connected in some way by lines, she said. Or were they? This would be my next avenue of investigation.

5 The *Ceques* of Cuzco

At the end of his report to the National Geographic Society, Gerald Hawkins, after establishing a negative astronomical result at Nasca, prudently avoided speculation and tossed the ball back into the court of archaeologists and anthropologists.

The most general explanation, he said, placed Nasca in the category of a *wak'a* or spirit place.

It was a throwaway statement but it was based on evidence in the chronicles. The Jesuit Father Bernabé Cobo had explained in 1653: 'Idolatry gave rise to many *wak'as* and shrines.' All manner of spirits or supernatural powers apparently lived within these *wak'as*, sometimes good and often malevolent, though whether the spirit was a separate entity or the *wak'a* itself is not clear. And Father Cobo gave as one example: 'If after a thunderstorm a piece of stone or metal was discovered which was different from others of its type, they [the Indians] believed it had been sent to be adored.' Ancestors as spirits in different forms were also *wak'as* and, according to Father Cobo, ancestors were turned into a variety of objects, both animate and inanimate. He also confirmed that each province venerated its principal *wak'as* as the mainspring of its ancestry and lineage.

Father Cobo travelled extensively in South America. He was a careful observer and his chronicle *The History of the New World* is generally regarded by historians as a most reliable source. In 1599 as a boy of seventeen he arrived in Lima and began school at the Jesuit College of San Martín. Ten years later, as a priest, he reached the city of Cuzco, once the Inca capital, where he reported on *ceques* (pronounced 'sikh' is') or 'lines on which *wak'as* were placed in order, like holy stopping places, to be venerated by all'. At first glance the connection between piles of stones, probably ancient *wak'as*, and the lines as pathways seemed simple, a real breakthrough in my search. The *ceque* connection for Nasca was certainly not new: it had been made by Mejía Xesspe when, in an address to a group of Americanists in Lima in 1939, he

Mejía Xesspe.

proposed that the lines were *ceques*, or sacred pathways. Dr Hans Hork-heimer had been less specific, but had suggested that the Nasca lines were used in some form of ritualistic ancestor worship.

Mejía Xesspe had worked with Alfred Kroeber when the Nasca lines were discovered in 1926. My next step was to visit him in his retire-ment in Lima. The taxi driver weaved a nerve-shattering route through the evening traffic to a residential street close to downtown Lima. As I rang the bell and waited, the familiar cross-cultural sound of a television commentator following a football match drifted through an open window, accompanied by a crescendo of cheering, passionate shouts of 'gol – Peru', and then deafening roars of approval. All the car drivers began hooting.

The door was opened by the elderly archaeologist, a surprisingly agile man with broad shoulders. I explained my presence and my interest in Nasca. He adjusted his spectacles.

'We'll go up to my study – come this way.'

I nodded a greeting to the football supporters. Mejía Xesspe waved a hand as a general introduction. 'It's the World Cup – an eliminating round or something like that,' he muttered as we climbed two flights of stairs.

We talked about Nasca and his work before turning to his opinion of the lines. 'What is a Nasca *ceque*?' I asked, little realizing that it would be the first of many such questions.

Mejía elaborated.

'It was some kind of path made for religious use – and the Nasca lines were paths or avenues.'

I needed to know if *ceques* led in straight lines, like the most obvious Nasca lines, or if they had bends or followed a zigzag form. Father Cobo had not confirmed these points, and now I pressed the archaeologist to explain.

'I also believe that *ceques* were rows of stones,' he said, emphasizing straight rows – and suggesting they were like boundaries.

Mejía Xesspe classified the Nasca markings into two groups: the long furrow-like lines and the wide avenues. He reasoned that as they were mostly near cemeteries at the edges of various valleys they were built for a religious purpose. He concluded by saying that each valley in the Nasca region had its own area of lines and then named a number of sites I had already visited. Another sixteenth-century chronicler, Juan Polo de Ondegardo, had noted *ceques* in Cuzco and *wak'as* around many highland villages in the Andes.

A seventeenth-century dictionary of Quechua, the Indian language, compiled by Gonçález Holguín, defined *ceqque* in Spanish as '*línea término*' or a boundary or limiting line. An equally old dictionary of Aymara, another Indian language, gives a simple translation – 'line'. If *ceques* were just boundaries or lines, why had Father Cobo and other chroniclers attributed a religious meaning to the word *ceque*? Were they just a simple means of making an orderly arrangement of the *wak'as*? (Gerald Hawkins had once suggested that the Nasca lines might be some form of locating grid.) As *ceque* was the only reference of any kind in the chronicles suggesting lines, my search had to begin with Father Cobo's famous chronicle:

History of the New World. 1653. Book 13, chapter 13.

'Del templo del sol salían, como de centro, ciertas lineas, que los indios llaman Ceques.'

Father Cobo's words were explicit. 'From the Temple of the Sun, as a centre, certain *lines* go outwards which the Indians call *Ceques*.' His manuscript was first transcribed 240 years later by the great Spanish historian Jiménez de la Espada, who added the following footnote using spelling copied from Holguín: '*Zeqque* – in Quechua, line or mark, boundary, limit, route, or direction.'

The Temple of the Sun, I knew, was in the old Inca capital of Cuzco, but there was nothing to indicate the precise nature of *ceques*. Every interpretation of the word was a clue of paramount significance. On the one hand, Father Cobo seemed to indicate that *ceques* were lines, while Mejía Xesspe had also described them as 'pathways or roads'. By the same token, the word 'line' is used to describe the markings at Nasca, although the many experts I spoke to, including Duncan Masson and Gerald Hawkins, more often referred to them as paths or roadways. Indeed, even Maria Reiche, in her *Mystery on the Desert*, spoke of them as 'ornamental pathways'.

Father Cobo's original manuscript is kept in the Columbina library in Seville.

It is easy to understand the widespread and general use of the term 'Nasca lines' because that is how they most certainly appear from the air when any sense of their true width is lost. But on the ground the narrow 'lines' appear as paths – shallow concave depressions below the level of the cleared surface, as if scoured by the wind or worn as a path. In fact the film I had made in 1963 – probably the first television documentary to describe the phenomena – was to a large extent responsible for perpetuating the use of the word 'lines'.

This semantic confusion gave an added impetus to my search for a possible relationship between *ceques* and the 'Nasca lines'. I was aware, however, of two immediate problems. The first was that while the Nasca lines were generally attributed to people of the adjacent valleys whose culture survived until approximately A.D. 500, the *ceques* apparently belonged to the Incas who dominated the Andes of Peru more than 700 years later, and then only for a relatively short time, from A.D. 1200 to 1532. More specifically, the organization of the *ceques* described by Father Cobo was ascribed to the ninth Inca Emperor – Pachacuti Yupanqui (A.D. 1438–71).

My second problem was that I knew from previous visits to Cuzco – the first was in 1961 – that lines in the form of those on the desert *pampa* did not exist in the historic Andean city. For this reason some twentieth-century archaeologists and historians have referred to *ceques* as 'invisible lines', or 'arbitrary', sometimes 'imaginary' or even 'lines of force' which radiated from the Temple of the Sun.

There is no doubt about the authenticity of Father Cobo's manuscript, as he had taken the information directly from reliable earlier sources, including Polo de Ondegardo who reached Cuzco within twenty-six years of the Spanish conquest. Polo made a diagram of the distribution of the '*zeqques* and shrines' for priests studying the ancient religion. Several copies were made, but all seem to have been lost. Until 1973 it was also generally assumed that Father Cobo's original seventeenth-century manuscript was lost. Then Dr Roland Hamilton, a linguist from the University of San José, California, identified it while researching ancient documents in the Colombina Library in Seville.

In Father Cobo's time, Cuzco was a fine, compact city set in a steep fertile valley high in the Andes. The Temple of the Sun or Coricancha (meaning 'golden enclosure') stood on a levelled bluff between two small rivers, the Huatanay and Tullumayo. The *ceques* apparently extended in all directions, some as far as twelve miles, constructed, supposedly, by clearing the hardy vegetation, mostly coarse grass.

An early seventeenth-century impression of Cuzco from a manuscript by G. Braun and Franz Hogenburg.

I reasoned that if Father Cobo had seen *ceques* or paths in Cuzco in 1609, then there could be two or perhaps three reasons to account for their disappearance and current 'invisibility'. Most likely of all could be the effect of more than three and a half centuries of plant growth; if the paths had fallen into disuse, the mountain sides would fairly quickly return to their natural state. Later, as Cuzco grew, the land would have been used, with animals tended there and patches ploughed for cultivation. In more recent decades, of course, they would have disappeared beneath the new city suburbs that are quickly extending over all the lower levels of the valley.

Another explanation for the disappearance of the lines or paths could have been political. In the early seventeenth century the Spanish Church in Peru instructed its priests to destroy any symbol of the ancient religion, especially the *wak'as* or sacred shrines. One account from the time of the Viceroy Montesclaros says that 600 idols from Huarochirí were burned in Lima's public square and an Indian idolater was flogged in the Viceroy's presence. In the years 1617 and 1618 idol and witch hunts were legion. Records show that in one coastal area alone 6,000 people confessed to idolatry, 679 sorcerers were discovered and 603 principal *wak'as* were removed with 3,418 *conopas* (mostly small stones or unusually shaped pebbles believed by the Indians to

house the family ancestor – these were the *penates* of the Indians). At the same time the priests confiscated 617 mummies as evidence of ancestor worship. All over Peru, the Spanish clergy had native priests and sorcerers arrested. *Wak'a* worship was treated more severely than drunkenness, and ritual musical instruments and costumes were destroyed. So aggressive was the 'Extirpation' that Indians tried to hide many of their most sacred relics. One anthropologist suggested to me that the *ceques* might have been destroyed by the Indians in order to prevent the discovery of their *wak'as*.

The Nasca valley was depopulated by the time the 'Extirpation' began and consequently would not have attracted the attention of the Spanish priests. Thus I began to realize that all the paraphernalia of broken pots, stones, shell and animal bones I had seen on the *pampa*, or knew from Maria Reiche's and Dr Horkheimer's early descriptions, could have been associated with Nasca *wak'as* which, by a strange twist of fate, had survived the campaign against idolatry. By the time people settled in Nasca again, the 'Extirpation' was over, and sometime near 1660 Catholicism had become integrated into Indian life.

Whatever the reason, *ceques* as lines are no longer visible in Cuzco. A number of *wak'as* are still there, however, and so I decided my next stop should be the old Inca capital high in the Andes. On a humid misty morning, with the temperature touching 70°F., I climbed the steps under the tail of a Faucett Boeing 727 for the fifty-minute flight from Lima to Cuzco. I had asked special permission to follow the route from the flight deck in preparation for shooting a documentary film. Soon after take-off a stewardess checked my credentials and Captain Ramirez called me to the cabin.

At 2,000 feet we cleared the last wisps of the coastal fog and I looked out towards the massively rugged slopes of the western Andes and somewhere, among the foothills, the Nasca *pampa*. Everywhere was parched and brown, and only in the depths of a deep canyon did a trickle of water catch some sunlight and shimmer momentarily. We passed beyond it and headed south-east to where a bank of high cumulus cloud lay over wetter, more fertile mountains. Tiny squares of cultivated land clung to the hillsides as patches on a quilt. Then, as we climbed steeply to 30,000 feet, the ground seemed to reach up to touch the 'plane. We were above the massive bulk of the Andes and ranges more than 20,000 feet high lay in breathtaking rows on either side. Ahead lay more high mountains and tiny lakes with mirror-like surfaces, dark silvery-blue. As we headed into the former Inca stronghold,

Corpus Christi in Cuzco. Solemn religious occasions and elaborate processions are part of the Andean life.

Machu Picchu.

the only sign of life was a smudge of dust left behind by a truck on a mountain road. Captain Ramirez, relaxed and informal, pointed to the landmarks.

'On clear days you can see to the Amazon from here.'

I peered eastwards.

'Sometimes we see the forests.' He checked his gauge. 'Now we're over the River Apurimac. It's said to be the main source of the Amazon, over 4,000 miles from the mouth.' Somewhere below had been the Inca bridge immortalized by Thornton Wilder in *The Bridge of San Luis Rey*. Then, a few minutes later, Captain Ramirez pointed to another deep gorge slipping silently below. It was a place I knew well.

Many years before I had travelled the Urubamba by raft, dropping 15,000 feet through thundering white-crested rapids from the Andes to the Amazon – another journey with Mark Howell. On the way we had stopped at Machu Picchu, the Inca town the Spanish soldiers never discovered. Hiram Bingham, an American explorer, reached it in July 1911, and found temples, fountains and its *intihuatana*, carved from solid granite, intact. He called the place the Lost City of the Incas, a name which has stuck.

Our flight approached Cuzco from the north, across the flat plain of Anta (meaning 'copper'), a famous Inca battlefield. A minute more and the ground fell away sharply leaving us suspended over the city. On our left, as we entered the Cuzco valley, stood the massive hand-shaped boulders of the Sacsahuaman 'fortress' built by Pachacuti Inca Yupanqui. Beside it a giant white-painted statue of Christ with outstretched arms overlooked the red-tiled city.

Minutes later the aircraft banked and turned before making a perfect touchdown. Somewhat unwillingly, I let two young lads argue about my baggage and transfer it to a vintage Dodge finely tuned for the altitude – the airport itself is 11,000 feet. We reached the Government Tourist Hotel in a record time of ten minutes. A small notice beside my bed from the *gerente*, or management, advised guests 'to rest and avoid exertion' immediately upon arrival in the rarefied mountain atmosphere. As I retained some acclimitization from an earlier visit, I felt no ill effects, though headaches and breathlessness are symptoms of what Peruvians call *soroche* or mountain sickness. In the restaurant I ordered a *maté de coca*, an infusion like good British tea, but made with coca leaves: its mild properties seem to help counter the effects of the thin Andean air, and as a brew it usually surpasses the local coffee.

Pukamarka – once a large shrine in the heart of Inca Cuzco. It was the second *wak'a* of the fifth *ceque* in the Chinchasuyu. Also it was the second *wak'a* of the sixth *ceque* in the same quarter. Today, it houses a cinema.

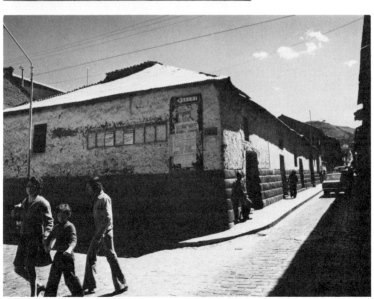

Next I walked to the central square or the Plaza de Armas, once the Huacaypata (leisure) square of the Incas. The massive seventeenth-century cathedral now stands on the north-east side, the fine baroque church of the Company of Jesus is on the south-east, and low colonnades, mostly from the colonial period, surround the north-west and west. The square was crowded. The Cuzqueños, dressed typically in their dark suits and fedora hats, mingled with tourists of many nationalities. A group of students were campaigning vociferously as I squeezed between wooden stalls piled high with oranges. On the steps of the cathedral two Quechua Indians sat deep in conversation, while their dark eyes watched every move I made. They were wearing the fine, hand-woven ponchos of Paucartambo, a tiny village in a mountain valley thirty-one miles to the north. To them Cuzco probably seemed as far from home as London was for me.

To reach the Temple of the Sun I turned south-east from the square. Down a narrow street named Loreto, I came across original Inca walling on either side, still in excellent condition. When the Spanish reached Cuzco in 1533 much of the central part of the city was built from these perfectly cut blocks of dull-brown rock fitted together without cement. In those days the buildings were low and thatched. While their walls were resilient to the shocks of earthquakes, they were at the same time solid and they are continuing evidence of the Inca achievement.

The street runs straight and leads in the direction of the temple with such apparent purpose that it could have been one of the *ceques* I was looking for. Before reaching the temple, Loreto crosses another street near a large area enclosed by numerous Inca-built walls. This was Pukamarca, one of the principal temples of ancient Cuzco and apparently an ancient *wak'a* where, according to Father Bernabé Cobo, a god known as Chucuyulla 'made a loud noise'. The cinema, with which modern Cuzco has replaced the temple, was maintaining these traditions: within the once hallowed walls a western – *un gran estréño* (a great show) – was careering to its noisy climax.

Part of the great charm of Cuzco lies in the many narrow streets like Loreto, where Inca stonework provides the foundations for several centuries of building. The Spanish began by building churches and since then a new city has grown, largely following the original street plan. A Dominican monastery and church of grey stone, built sometime after 1650, now encloses the ruined walls of the Temple of the Sun. In Inca days an open space, the *Inti-* (or sun-) *pampa*, lay to the north-east of the temple, and it remains as a small, attractive but noisy square where buses stop full of tourists from all over the world. Originally the Temple stood on a flattened, well-prepared site overlooking the Huatanay and Tullumayo rivers. To the south-west, a steep slope overlooks modern Cuzco's main street, the Avenue of the Sun, and Inca engineers supported the hillside with a curved retaining wall they extended eastwards for over eighty feet. The apse of the present church stands above the curve of the wall, which is among the finest Inca work in Cuzco. Probably the stones were dressed in place, but were fitted together without mortar and the spaces between them are so microscopic that paper cannot be slipped between them.

Chroniclers describing the temple in the sixteenth century recount many colourful stories, some of doubtful accuracy. Perhaps the most

Hatunrumiyoc – the place of a large twelve-angled stone on the Inca way to the Antisuyu, the north-eastern part of the empire.

The curved retaining wall built by the Incas' engineers, probably to strengthen the natural platform on which they sited the Coricancha or 'golden enclosure' of the Temple of the Sun.

detailed account was written by Garcilaso de la Vega, *el Inca*, born in Cuzco in 1539, son of a Spanish captain (himself the illegitimate son of a nobleman) and the niece of Huayna Capac, the eleventh Inca. Garcilaso left Cuzco twenty-one years later and wrote his monumental *Royal Commentaries* in Spain. The third book of the *Commentaries* was completed sometime before 1603 and leaves no doubt that a magnificent Hall of the Sun stood at the front of the temple: beyond it and arranged around a court, the Incas had four 'chapels' which Garcilaso accorded to other deities, the moon, the stars, the thunder and the rainbow. A fifth room was used by the priests.

The stonework must have been impressive, judging from Garcilaso's memories of its very 'fine and polished stones' and the few remains of Inca walls still standing within the cool monastery cloister. Of the unique Hall of the Sun, there is not a trace, and the most likely explanation for its disappearance is that it was demolished when the Dominican church was built.

The Temple of the Sun was the most ancient, most sacred and most richly adorned of the Inca shrines. In May 1533, Francisco Pizarro, then in Cajamarca, a mountain town over 680 miles to the north-west, sent three soldiers to Cuzco to make a report of the value of the gold in the city and, no doubt, to study its defences. They stayed in Cuzco a week, watched all the time by Quizquiz, the general of Inca Atahuallpa. As they discovered, the Sun Temple or Coricancha 'measured 300 paces from corner to corner and was sheathed in gold – altogether 700 plates were removed and each weighed over 4 lb.' At 180 dollars an ounce this would be valued at very roughly eight million US dollars in today's terms.

All the walls of the Hall of the Sun were hung with plaques of gold and according to Garcilaso a golden disc, covering one wall entirely, represented the sun in the form of a face surrounded by rays and long tongues of flame. On either side of the sun disc the mummies of past Incas were seated on thrones of gold. Each mummy, also a *wak'a*, was hidden by the Indians before the main Spanish force arrived. Since those days much of the interior of the Temple of the Sun has been destroyed, by Spanish soldiers and by later builders. Then in May 1950 an earthquake, one of a series over the centuries, severely damaged the church and monastery. A team of experts and craftsmen was raised to piece together the ruins and excavate some previously unknown parts

From the centre of the present courtyard within the old Inca walls of the Temple of the Sun, Dr Chávez Ballón explains his map of the *ceques*.

The Lion in the mountains. The Inca city of Cuzco was built roughly in the shape of a puma, an important feline divinity. The fortress of Sacsahuaman was at the head and the Great Plaza – Huacaypata was under the breast.

of the Inca temple. I had come to see one member of this team, Dr Manuel Chávez Ballón who, as the professor of archaeology at Cuzco University and a leading authority on Inca Cuzco, has spent many years tracing the *ceques* and the *wak'as*. We had corresponded and he had promised to show me the *wak'as* in order that I might map them to see if they lay in straight lines.

When I arrived at the heavy iron-studded door of the monastery, I asked an attendant to direct me to Dr Chávez's office. 'Is he expecting you? He's showing some friends around the city,' he said. As the time

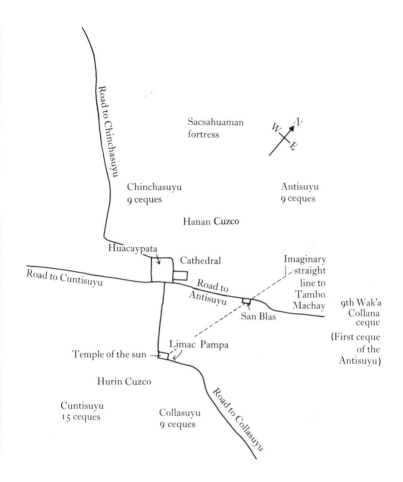

was close to twelve noon, the Cuzco lunch hour, I decided to wait. In less than five minutes I was asked by several passers-by if they could help – perhaps to direct me somewhere? When I explained the reason for my visit, their faces lit up.

'Ah maestro Chávez' (meaning the 'expert'). They nodded knowingly, leaving me to speculate where he might be. At 12.30 he arrived, hurrying with a long narrow roll of papers under his arm. I introduced myself.

'As you know, I want to find out about *ceques*.'

He hesitated for a moment, looking for somewhere to leave his papers before deciding he would carry them after all.

'Come this way – we'll start now.'

We agreed to have lunch at a nearby restaurant whose menu was written on a small blackboard outside the door.

Dr Chávez is known to every historian who has worked in Cuzco. I should have realized he was no typical university professor having been advised to 'think Andean' by more than one of his friends. In fact he has all the features of Andean descent. His once dark, now greying, hair was carefully brushed and like many Cuzceños he had a neatly clipped moustache. Every sentence he punctuated with some hint of many years in the Inca capital – a nod to a friend across the room or a smile for an old student.

Our four-course meal was very typical of mountain Peru: mutton with maize soup, crisp pork with lightly spiced small potatoes (the potato came from the Andes and many varieties grow wild), a jelly-like *mazamorra* or purple maize starch (a very traditional Peruvian dish), and we rounded it off with another, stronger, *maté de coca*. On earlier visits to Cuzco I had seen the museums and ruins, and visited the Cathedral, but that lunch with Dr Chávez added a fascinating and new dimension to the history.

'You know of the *ceques* from Father Cobo, don't you?'

I nodded.

'Well, Cobo says the Temple of the Sun was the centre. As you will find out it doesn't always work out that way.'

I had to know more.

'How were the *ceques* arranged and – what precisely is a *ceque*?' I asked.

'Let's have another *maté*,' suggested the archaeologist and he spoke in Quechua to a buxom young girl wearing a neat white apron: she was only a few generations removed from her Inca ancestry. I caught the word 'Inglaterra' as he pointed to my cup. From her cheery smile I guessed Dr Chávez had said something about my unexpected taste for *maté*. He reached to the centre of the table to a glass holding several clean table-napkins.

'This will do. I'll draw you a plan.'

He marked the Temple of the Sun. Then he drew two lines crossing at right angles with the temple at the centre point. 'Cuzco was divided into four quarters – the quarters extended into the Inca Empire – the Tawantinsuyu.'

Then he drew more lines, each one radiating from the Temple of the Sun.

'These are the forty-one *ceques* listed by Cobo, perhaps forty-two. Nine to each of three of the quarters and fourteen for the south-western quarter or Cuntisuyu.'

The finished diagram resembled the spokes of a cartwheel, and I immediately thought of the 'star-like centres' at Nasca where lines radiated (or, as I believed, converged) on hills and stone piles.

'These are the *ceques* – a diagram only. We don't know the form of the *ceques*.' He made the point strongly, and continued: 'Each *ceque* was in the charge of an *ayllu* – a family or kinship group.' Then he reminded me of Father Cobo again, quoting: ' "The *wak'as* were placed on the lines like holy stopping places" – like knots on a string. But we'll see that later.'

Each *ceque* had between four and fifteen *wak'as* placed on it and each was individually named and described by Cobo.

My immediate reaction was to consider the possibility of tracing the *wak'as*. That would reveal the plan of the 'lines' and if they had been straight it would be obvious. Almost everything or every part of the old city could be identified and Dr Chávez knew over half of the total of 328 *wak'as* detailed in Father Cobo's list – temples, single stones, groups of stones, fountains, hills, places for idols, sacrifices, ancient gods, spirits and demons of all kinds. It seemed that many of these *wak'as* had not been totally destroyed by the Spanish. In fact, in places where they existed as buildings, many had been re-used, and served as foundations for newer constructions, as was the case with the Temple of the Sun: only the idols, gold and other sacred objects had been removed by the *conquistadores*.

I asked Dr Chávez if he had located all the *wak'as* on any one *ceque*. His answer was disappointing. He had not and no single *ceque* was complete. 'Unfortunately many of the names have changed,' he said. Then, referring to Cobo's manuscript again, he explained that though each *ceque* was in the care of a family group, there were many good reasons to suspect that some families possessed land, and hence *wak'as*, well away from their own *ceque* which, if it were a path, would not be one straight line but could be a zigzag.

How, I wondered, could this information relate to Nasca? Initially it did not seem to do so. There was no evidence that *ceques* ran in straight lines but then I remembered that although Gerald Hawkins and other experts had been concerned with the straight lines on the desert *pampa* because they were the most obvious features, other lines have a zigzag form and a few, after continuing in a straight line, bend sharply and afterwards continue straight again. Stone piles usually mark the bends.

When Mejía Xesspe put forward his *ceque* theory for Nasca in 1939, he suggested that the lengths of the paths there were determined by the space they could fill: the longest lines led across relatively flat *pampa*, while in places where the terrain was hilly, only relatively few lines extended any great distance. Many of the Nasca lines, in fact, are short, or have the form of a grid. As Maria Reiche explained to me, walking along the total length of a grid can take an hour, as the lines are joined by transverse paths at each end, thus forming one long, tortuous route. I had a hunch that *ceques* in Cuzco might similarly have formed one long continuous path from *wak'a* to *wak'a* (which was in fact one step nearer to the answer than I realized at the time).

Also, why were the Cuzco *wak'as* now mostly within the town? The opposite was true of Nasca where the piles of stones, gullies and hilltops I had seen on the desert always lay well beyond the edge of any

Idols and *wak'as* of the Collasuyus. Indians offer a black llama at a shrine. In this drawing made in about 1615, Felipe Guamán Poma, a minor official, identifies the animal as 'a sheep'. The name was commonly misused by early chroniclers.

former settlements. Dr Chávez picked up this point and emphasized that Cuzco would have been much smaller in the sixteenth century and the most distant *wak'as* listed certainly extended the *ceques* well into the countryside.

One sure comparison I felt could be drawn between the two sites was based on an analysis of the form of *wak'as* in Cuzco. It showed that more than half of the holy shrines were stones, many were hills – or stones on hills – and some were described as 'open places' (reminiscent of the trapezoidal clearings on the desert *pampa*) where Father Cobo said ceremonies were held. Sometimes small animals were sacrificed, sometimes llamas or even children. At certain *wak'as* Father Cobo explained how the Indians made offerings of coca and sea shells (again, I remembered shells at Nasca). Of one *wak'a* Father Cobo states: 'In this hill they make a (universal) sacrifice of young boys and girls and small figures in gold; also they burn clothes and llamas as befits such a holy shrine.'

Human sacrifice was the most valuable offering that could be made and such sacrifices were generally performed in times of great need: famine, epidemics or disaster in war. Also Inca ceremonial occasions often involved ritual sacrifices and at one 'coronation' 200 children were slaughtered: they were selected for their perfection, like the animals used in lesser sacrifices. The children had to walk around the *wak'a* three times. The older ones were made drunk on *chicha*, a maize beer, and then, after being strangled with a cord, their hearts were cut out to be offered, still beating, to the blood-spattered shrine. In another ceremony priests smeared human blood across the heads of ancestors' mummies.

The only signs of sacrifices at Nasca were the tiny animal bones reported by Padre Rossel Castro, the Nasca priest in the 1940s, but there was no reason to suspect that anything, either flesh or bones, would remain to be identified. As well as children, animals, particularly the small native Andean cavies or guinea pigs, were offered frequently at the *wak'as*, and I suspected that the small bones seen by the Padre at Nasca had belonged to cavies.

To pursue a comparison between the *ceques* and the Nasca lines I asked Dr Chávez about the hills of the Cuzco *ceques*. Were all the hills visible from the Temple of the Sun? At Nasca, the hills at the ends of some lines are prominent features in a flat area and, like Mejía Xesspe and Dr Horkheimer, I had noticed that such lines often began at the very edge of the desert plateaux directly above old cemeteries or settle-

Huanacauri, a hill to the south-east of the city, is the most sacred *wak'a* in all the Inca Empire after the Temple of the Sun. Thick mountain grass conceals the few ruins.

ments, and could have been paths to a shrine. In Cuzco the *ceques* led from the Temple, the central holy place, to surrounding *wak'as*, of which hills were often the most distant shrines.

Dr Chávez recommended a view over the city. After lunch we took a longer route back to the Temple of the Sun and he pointed out many shrines on the way. On arriving at his office, he led the way to an upper floor of the monastery where he introduced me to the Prior, Father Rosas Rodríguez, who held the key to the bell tower.

Together we made our way through dusty lofts filled with carved and gilded wood standing ready to be replaced as reconstruction proceeded. Dr Chávez stepped carefully on a temporary catwalk of narrow planks to reach a door and, still holding his roll of papers, fumbled with a key. After a few moments he opened the door and revealed another room leading to more steps.

'From here you get the best view of Cuzco and the hills around the city,' he said breathlessly. He ducked under a bell-rope and from a stone platform pointed out the four quarters or *suyus* of ancient Cuzco.

The city lies in a valley sloping gently to the south-east. My attention was drawn to the mountainous western horizon and Dr Chávez named several of the high places – on one summit a cross had been set. He explained that such places were still regarded as holy places, like other *wak'as* around the city.

I asked if offerings were still made there.

'No – not these days.' He was thoughtful. 'Times are changing quickly around here. You may find the old customs hang on in some of the villages, but now in Cuzco we have a modern city.'

Looking down the valley I watched a tiny red pencil of an Aero Peru Fokker jet taking off from the airport. No sound from its engines reached us. Dr Chávez pointed to a hill with three peaks dwarfing the plane and standing out among the ridges to the south-east of the city.

'That's Huanacauri' (pronounced 'Whana'cowri'), 'which was the most sacred *wak'a* in all the Inca Empire, after the Temple of the Sun.' Dr Chávez had been to the summit and said that though it was not very high, it was hard work to get to the top.

'What's there? Is it worth the effort?' I wanted to know, as there would be many other shrines to visit, and my time in Cuzco was limited to two or perhaps three weeks at the most.

'Some ruins, not very impressive and badly destroyed by the weather.' Dr Chávez implied that I would be wasting my time, and suggested the chronicles would give me a good account of the shrine in Inca times.

Father Cobo, in his list of *ceques*, placed Huanacauri as the seventh *wak'a* on the sixth *ceque* of the Collasuyu or south-east quarter. It was, he said, the 'hill where they made the most sacrifices'. Cobo added that the Indians worshipped a rough, spindle-shaped stone which they said represented Ayar Cachi, one of the brothers of the first Inca, Manco Capac. 'It stood on top of the hill and before the Spanish arrived many festivals were held there – the Spaniards took a great quantity of gold and silver from the shrine and, so it seems, did not notice the stone.'

'Have the Huanacauri ruins been excavated – and has any more gold been found?' I queried. After all, I reckoned the Spanish had been first lured to Peru by the gold. Dr Chávez laughed good-humouredly: archaeologists are always amused by the layman's obsession with gold and treasure.

'There's nothing there now. Test excavations were made some time ago and all we found was broken pottery.'

I decided, somewhat reluctantly, not to climb Huanacauri.

From the bell tower of Santo Domingo church, above the old temple, I searched the hillsides for lines or paths. Most of the old city boundaries have been smothered by suburbs and modern roads edging outwards and up the steep slopes. Beyond the suburbs the land is cultivated, while higher still there is nothing but wild mountain grass. I could see no sign of a straight path or track, even in the direction of Huanacauri, and yet the chronicles give a clear account of races that were held along tracks leading from that shrine.

Races were significant Inca ceremonies. A suggestion that the Nasca lines might have been used as 'race tracks' had been made to me once at a meeting of the Andean Society in London. Similar paths through the forests of Brazil are still used for races in which the men (and women) of different family units compete by running carrying heavy logs. The most famous of the ancient Cuzco races was held at the boys' puberty festival: after sacrifices of llamas had been made first at Huanacauri and then in the Great Plaza, the boys raced recklessly down another steep hill, Anahuarque. At the 'finishing post', young maidens are said to have 'waited upon them with vases of maize beer'.

Using false-colour and black and white infra-red film, I took the opportunity to photograph the sides of the valley, hoping to reveal any differences in the vegetation along any old paths; but when processed later, the photographs revealed nothing more than strangely coloured fields and magenta trees. (The season of the year is important for using this type of photography successfully. It is possible that the plant growth was not at the best stage when I took the pictures.)

Dr Chávez raised one arm and stretched it out in a straight line from his eye. 'Look at the churches,' he said, pointing to a tower about a mile away. 'Many of them are built on the sites of old *wak'as*. When the Spanish destroyed the Inca shrines they replaced them with their own churches.'

I followed the direction of his arm. Many church towers and cupolas stood above the red-tiled roofs of the city and, looking beyond the tower, Dr Chávez had indicated a hill surmounted by a small cross which was also in line. The other churches appeared to have no particular alignment from the Temple of the Sun, though later I was shown a line of five churches and one shrine that stood clearly in a straight line crossing the Plaza de Armas from east to west of the city.

Father Cobo records how, 500 years ago, many shrines or *wak'as* surrounded Sacsahuaman, a massive fortress standing in the hills above Cuzco. 20,000 men laboured for thirty years to complete the work of moving, shaping and placing the massive limestone blocks – some weigh over 100 tons.

I examined the results so far. In Cuzco, at first count, I had managed only two, or at the most three, straight lines of shrines out of a total of forty-two *ceques*. Of those, two lines met at the Plaza de Armas, not the Temple of the Sun, which Father Cobo had said was the centre point of the *ceques*. The *plaza* and the temple are over a quarter of a mile apart.

Dr Chávez knew that I was searching for straight lines like those of Nasca and he shook his head emphatically.

'There is nothing in the documents to say the *ceques* were straight and some, in my opinion, are definitely not.' He laid out a map from his roll and indicated some *wak'as* which were listed as appearing on two different *ceques*. 'That kind of situation is difficult to sort out,' he said, referring to my suggestion that by pinpointing the shrines in modern Cuzco, I would find a set of straight lines. 'Another problem is the size of the shrines.' I guessed what he was going to say. 'Look at Pukamarka – over 300 yards by 300 yards, almost any line would fall somewhere in that space.'

On the following afternoon I set out for one shrine which I knew I could locate with certainty in the hills to the east. Tambo Machay is a well-preserved Inca site about five miles from the city and a favourite stopping-place for tourists. I tagged on the end of a group of French students from Nantes, the leader of their group offering me a place in their bus for the fifteen-minute ride. The route to Tambo Machay took us out of the Cuzco valley along a newly completed asphalt road, passing between small fields scratched from hillsides of grey stone. The potato harvest was near and the country people, many of them of almost pure Indian descent, were tending neat rows of surprisingly robust plants. Purple lupin-like flowers brightened the tangle of roadside undergrowth and a barrage of clicking cameras greeted the sight of a llama being led by a small boy. The villagers themselves were well used to tourists and one old lady waved a woollen sweater at the speeding vehicle, with the same impassive face of a matador using his cape. 'Comprame,' she called, meaning 'Buy from me.'

Tambo Machay, today, consists of four walls of Inca stonework set into a hillside. In the top wall four small trapezoidal niches that probably once held idols or other *wak'as* face eastwards into the valley, while below them crystal clear water dances through open channels. From Father Cobo's description Tambo Machay appears to have been a sort of hunting lodge belonging to the Inca Yupanqui. The house itself was a shrine and 'all kinds of sacrifices were made there, apart from children'. A nearby spring was also sacred, and a third *wak'a*, part of the same house, consisted of a fountain with two sources of running water where 'they made many sacrifices in addition to children'. These *wak'as*, said Father Cobo, were the ninth, eighth and tenth on the first *ceque* of the north-eastern or Anti quarter.

There was still more than three hours of daylight left, so with a photocopy of Father Cobo's chronicle in my hand I decided to try to follow the route of the second *ceque* of the Anti quarter, which ran from a hill near to Tambo Machay back into the centre of Cuzco and to the Temple of the Sun. To find the farthest end of the *ceque* I had to locate the ninth *wak'a*, called Cascasayba, which was described by Cobo as 'certain stones on a hill where all things including children were offered'. Cobo said the hill was known as Quisco. I questioned the bus driver, the custodian of the ruins and two workmen (obviously

Tambo Machay.

locals) who were watching the French photographers at work, but none could tell me anything about the hill. Puzzled, I looked around me until I saw high above me a simple cross. It looked disturbingly small standing on a high point of the ridge, but it seemed a promising place from which to start my search. If I were really lucky, maybe the cross would mark the spot of the ancient shrine.

The first stage was simple: a planked bridge crossed a narrow stream to a grassy, though boggy, slope leading to the foot of the hill which I estimated would be a 500-foot climb. I skirted a crudely built llama corral before reaching the tough part. It was hard going and I had to make several long detours across steep, precipitous outcrops of rock. Eventually, puffing hard (the altitude must have been over 12,000 feet), I reached a level grassy ridge several yards wide that ran almost due north–south linking several individual summits. Cuzco was just visible in the valley and beyond it, to the south-west, the grassy summit of

On the second *ceque* of the Antisuyu.

Huanacauri shone yellow-green against a leaden sky.

The cross in front of me, of the Latin form, had been made from
two rough wooden poles, one with a longer arm, crudely nailed together. Once it must have been painted black, but the paint was almost
gone and a scrap of cloth flapped loosely from one arm. The upright
pole was set among some grey stones, and a soot-blackened, empty
evaporated-milk can rested at the base, its tattered blue label bearing
the words 'Leche Gloria' – a local brand. I searched carefully without
disturbing anything until I noticed a few coca leaves wedged between

the stones. My heart leaped when I realized the *wak'a* was still respected: the leaves were not brown, but greyish-green, indicating they had not long been placed there.

I tested the alignments. From the cross I could see down to the ruins of Tambo Machay, where my companion students were preparing to leave, and beyond, to the Temple of the Sun in the Cuzco valley. Then disappointment: it was obvious that no straight line could be drawn between these three points. The cross must have been at least twenty-five degrees out of line.

I continued south along the ridge hoping to find a place where I could stand facing Cuzco and see the walls of Tambo Machay and the distant temple in a straight line. At that spot, I hoped to find some trace of another *wak'a*. After a ten-minute walk, I reached a level place with two low natural rock outcrops about a hundred yards apart. Could one of these be Cascasayba? Once again I was to be frustrated – this time the Temple of the Sun was out of sight, hidden behind trees on the rim of the valley.

I continued to the southernmost point of the ridge where I found another small pile of stones, neatly grouped, obviously with a purpose. Again it might have been the old *wak'a* or a much more recent structure. I felt I must be very close to the site of the *wak'a* but with the lengthening shadows of the setting sun now beginning to fall over the valley, I made the decision to head back towards Cuzco. The mountain air cooled quickly and I pulled my duvet tight. From my high viewpoint I could see the route I would follow to a point where I could meet the main road. The latter, I felt certain, followed the same directions as the *ceque*.

I was eager to see more of Father Cobo's *wak'as* if possible. The eighth holy place on the *ceque* was a fountain or spring 'where they made offerings of llamas, clothes and shells'; the seventh was an Inca resting place in a flat cleared area. Both were close to Tambo Machay and it was not long before I passed the site where they must have been. Once again I could not distinguish the location precisely as there were several places with running water. Then, heading back into rough ground again, I found another larger boulder topped with a cross, then a few yards beyond and still on my route, another boulder with three small angular stones on the flat surface. According to Father Cobo the other shrines of the *ceque* included two hills, one *wak'a* on the side of a hill, a specific large stone on which sacrifices were made and a place called Vilcacona – now a famous hotel in the heart of Cuzco. He said that at certain times of the year all the idols and *wak'as* of Cuzco were carried to Vilcacona, where sacrifices were made – 'it was a very holy shrine to which coca was offered'. Of these I could only trace Vilcacona. I arrived back in Cuzco at sunset convinced that my walk had proved that the second *ceque* of the north-eastern quarter was *not* a straight line.

Before leaving Lima I had called at the S.A.N. office to collect thirty-two air photographs of Cuzco and the region extending to Tambo Machay. That night in my hotel room I laid the shots on the one small and rather rickety table and aligned a ruler from the Temple of the Sun to the hill I had climbed. Vilcacona, the first *wak'a*, the Tambo Machay fountains and one flat part of the ridge of the hill aligned, yet still there was no sign of a path or line on the photographs. The negatives had been taken in June 1956, more than twenty years earlier.

In the course of the next two weeks, I followed more *ceques*, usually with the help of Dr Chávez. We walked the streets for miles; and if it rained, which luckily was not often, we took shelter in a shop or some friendly home along the way. We were always greeted affably: '*Buenos días*, doctor', or 'You're a stranger here these days, doctor', as we cringed from the downpour. The archaeologist would make a point of asking the shop owner for the *old* name for the place. Then he would quickly scribble the reply on his chart, a difficult task as the map, often in use as a cape, was fast becoming limp and unmanageable.

I soon learned that old *wak'as* can be found in every part of Cuzco: in places developed as diversely as hotels, offices, restaurants, bars, shops and private houses. When Dr Chávez and I once ate at a restaurant on a corner of the main *plaza*, seated beside some fine Inca walling (the local law is very conservation conscious), I wondered if the other diners realized that in the place where they now read their guide books, and chewed their Andean steaks, the Inca people had, according to Father Cobo, 'offered great sacrifices'. The exact form of the sacrifices was perhaps best left unsaid.

By the end of my search, and after numerous meals and litres of beer, I was forced to conclude that, generally, the shrines were not to be found on long straight lines. Neither is there historical evidence to prove that *ceques* were straight paths or lines. The precise meaning of the word *ceque* was as elusive as ever and a large question mark was left hanging over any interpretation of the Nasca lines as *ceques*.

Then what were the *ceques*? They had to be connected with the ancient religion or Father Cobo would not have referred to the shrines as 'holy stopping places on a *ceque*'. For lack of any other positive information I had to leave my search for their meaning and, hoping that new leads would turn up, turn my investigation to the shrines themselves.

6   The Shrines

All the chronicles said that *wak'as* were shrines venerated by the Indians, but did they have further significance and why had they been sited in specific places? Could they have been aligned with the rise of the sun or moon over the horizon? Were they observation places from which priests studied the stars? Or were they no more than areas where, in the Indian mind, spirits or gods resided?

Father Cobo wrote a careful account of the *wak'as* of Cuzco. He listed each by name, describing its form, the sacrificial offerings made there, position on the *ceque* and occasionally the purpose. According to Father Cobo, nearly half the Cuzco *wak'as* were stones and springs; hills and ceremonial clearings accounted for almost all of the remainder. Some of the shrines were landmarks, others boundary posts, a small number were places where 'sight of Cuzco was lost' and an even smaller number were, he said, specifically related to Inca astronomy.

Here then was a possible new lead in my investigation of the lines and stones of Nasca. Admittedly over a thousand years separate the earliest Nascas from the period when the *ceques* and *wak'as* of Cuzco were supposedly organized by Inca Pachacuti sometime after 1438. But this difference is insignificant in the broad sense because the veneration of stones and high places is an almost universal primitive cultural belief and still survives in some parts of the Andes today. Were the Nasca stones perhaps the shrines of the pre-Inca culture of the coastal desert?

When I first began to look for *wak'as* at Nasca I noticed stones of various sizes grouped meticulously in several different ways. As I became attuned to noticing the stones, I could distinguish many more. The most obvious collections were the large mounds, often six to ten

Of the 333 holy places on *ceques* listed by Father Cobo, over 80 were stones, more than 90 were springs and fountains. Specific landmarks, including caves, quarries, trees and deep gullies, numbered almost 50. Over 50 more were hills or hills with stones, while an assortment of meeting places, a jail and even a sacred root completed the total.

feet across and up to two to three feet high, built from relatively small stones. Common to many of the heaps was a depression in the top, possibly where a vessel or pole once stood – or made by latter-day treasure-hunters.

Next and perhaps the most numerous were smaller piles of stones, mostly in the cleared areas, often at intervals beside the lines and at the ends of some lines. Then there were large individual stones, either set singly or in groups. These did not resemble the huge megaliths of Europe but were smooth boulders of glacial or river-worked stone from one to two feet high. At the other extreme were the tiny stones: when I looked closely where lines appeared simply to fizzle out in the *pampa* I found, in fact, that stones were always there, often arranged in what appeared to be a haphazard way.

Other stones had been arranged in designs of several forms – half circles or a series of rectangles side by side or more complex patterns involving squares, half circles and rectangles. These patterns would be typically fifteen yards by four; not large relative to the dimensions of other features of the site. Similar arrangements of stones, more specifically circles of small stones and stones forming rectangular enclosures, were seen by Patricia Netherly near Collique. One of these stone designs at Nasca, first described by Maria Reiche, has two separate groups of ten contiguous rectangles. Another design similarly delimited

Valley

Plan

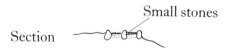

Stones

Disturbed

Small stones

Section

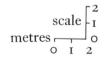

scale metres

2
1
0

0   1   2

A stone enclosure near Palpa, recorded by Hans Horkheimer in 1946, is now almost completely destroyed.

by rows of stones was drawn and meticulously photographed by Dr Hans Horkheimer as long ago as 1946. Nine 'compartments' were set in a row on the top of a hill above the Palpa valley just a few miles north of the Pampa de San José. When I visited the site, I found it badly disturbed, though many of the stones remained.

What then is the significance of the stones and other constructions at Nasca? Maria Reiche once said to me 'that every stone was important' and she always stressed that none should ever be moved. I remembered also Paul Kosok's early work. He had put forward two suggestions: that the heaps of stones could represent altars or possibly some kind of abacus-like counting device. I had asked Maria Reiche, on my most recent visit, for her latest opinion.

'Some people,' she said, hesitating slightly as if to catch a thought, 'some people think they have numerical significance.' She outlined her belief that some numbers were significant. 'Like seventy or seven, eighteen or fifty-four.'

So I had reached a new level in my investigation. I had read more than a hundred accounts, sometimes terrifying, often simple, of the ceremonies performed by the Incas at *wak'as*. Now I needed to delve into any other significance the shrines might have. In compiling all the expert advice I had received, the work seemed to divide itself into two strands. First, as both María Rostworowski and Gerald Hawkins had implied, I should look for the answer in the Indian mind, 'beyond the computer', and second, I should investigate the possible astronomical or calendric significance not of the lines this time but of the Cuzco *wak'as*. If this could be proved to be substantial, it might throw some light on the significance of the Nasca stones. I decided to deal with the astronomical or calendric possibility first.

This line of research seemed immediately promising. At least all the authorities appeared to accept that the Incas *had* a calendar. However, as I delved deeper I found that much of the material was contradictory. Almost predictably, the chroniclers were unclear on the subject; they are frequently accused of reticence on the subject of the Indians' apparent knowledge of astronomy. Very possibly, too, the chroniclers were simply confused. Even Father Cobo makes apparent errors: he lists forty-one *ceques* and implies that one of them was regarded as two – it was in two parts. Thus the total number of *ceques* is either forty-one or forty-two and not forty as he states in the summary at the end of his account. Other chroniclers give different totals of *wak'as*. All too often one chronicler simply lifted a story from another writer, stirred in some ideas which were probably European in origin, and presented a patently garbled report.

Any calendar based on the movement of the sun and moon has to take into account the difference between lunar months, averaging 29.53 days, and the solar year. Twelve lunar months come to 354.36 days and the tropical solar year is 365.2422 days: a difference of nearly eleven days (10.88). To reconcile these two 'years' and produce a workable calendar demands careful observation of the movements of both the sun and moon: not simply the work of a few years – that will not do. The observations have to be made critically over a period of several centuries.

The most widely accepted solution to this particularly ticklish problem is to insert extra months in accordance with a prescribed calendar 'round'. The Babylonian round was nineteen years and the Jewish calendar was developed from it. Our current Gregorian calendar was

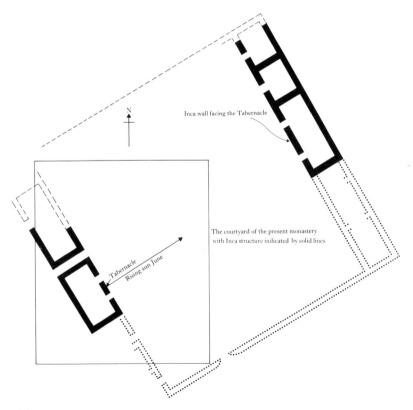

At the time of the June solstice the direct rays of the rising sun would have shone into this niche or 'tabernacle' to be reflected by plates of beaten gold and an array of precious stones.

introduced in 1582, but it does not take account of the moon. It is essentially a solar year, but it is accurate to within twenty-six seconds. I needed to know how the Inca calendar worked and how accurate it was.

The rotation of the earth and apparent movement of the skies was clearly significant to the Incas. The sun rose in the east and set in the west to an accompaniment of sacrifices and offerings to the gods, and the whole empire was divided into four quarters corresponding very approximately to the four cardinal directions. In Cuzco, the four quarters were defined more clearly and, according to one source, two *ceques* formed virtually due east–west lines.

Cuzco's Temple of the Sun. How was it aligned? Was it east–west, achieved by an equinox observation (or bisection of the rising and setting of a star on the northern horizon), or did it face another direction? I remembered Maria Reiche saying that her original interest in Andean astronomy had grown from the work of the German astronomer Rolf Müller. He wrote about Peruvian sun temples and their alignments in 1929, three years before Maria Reiche first arrived in Lima.

Rolf Müller found the front wall of a room in the temple to be aligned so as to point towards declination 23° 40′, which means it faces almost directly towards the June solstice. It was an alignment I felt I should investigate, so I arranged with Dr Chávez to visit the Temple. I used a detailed plan of the surviving Inca walls made by the eminent Americanist John Howland Rowe in 1941–2. Since Dr Rowe first visited Cuzco just before World War II, his life has been dedicated to the study of the Andean cultures, particularly the Inca. With his map as a guide I chose the room on the south-west side of the cloister of the present monastery, the same one that Müller had measured. Its stonework in perfect condition, the room is roughly thirty-eight feet by fifty feet and not a perfect rectangle. Its external east-facing wall contains a peculiar trapezoidal niche, or 'tabernacle' as the chronicler Garcilaso de la Vega called it, making a comparison with a Catholic altar. The interior of this 'tabernacle' is elaborately carved and a number of small holes and channels have survived the four and a half centuries since the arrival of the *conquistadores* in Cuzco.

Garcilaso described the tabernacle in the Temple of the Sun as sheathed with gold plates and set with many precious stones – 'emeralds and turquoise'. He said the Inca sat in the tabernacle when festivals of the sun were held. His account is confirmed by another chronicler, Pedro de Cieza de León, who visited Cuzco in 1550 and, the following year, wrote an account stating that the tabernacle was a seat which the 'sun struck as it rose'. It was a seat which only the king used; if anyone else did so 'the punishment was death'.

I set up a theodolite at the south-east outer corner of the room, and a student working on the reconstruction of the monastery held my ranging pole at the north-east corner some fifty feet away. Once the tiny tubular compass had settled, I checked the bearing along the line of the wall (336.5 degrees). I found that the wall with its tabernacle faced azimuth $336.5 + 90 = 426.5$, or azimuth 66.5 east of north. My measurement did not allow for the local magnetic variation, or the angular height of a hill to the east (newer buildings now obscure the view), but the result was close enough to show that the sun's rays would fall almost squarely on the wall at the time of the June solstice and obliquely at the equinox.

It is probable that the line of the foundation was fixed by a sunrise sighting before the other buildings were erected. The main surviving walls of the Temple appear to fit in a grid that points to the solstice sunrise. Once the main direction was obtained and laid down, it would have been fairly easy to strike off parallel lines and continue the grid, though which was the datum line may never be known.

One document implied that the Incas understood the difference

On the east side of the courtyard, the foundations for these Inca rooms were lower. The design feature might have been intended to allow the very first rays of dawn sunlight to bathe the tabernacle.

between solar and lunar years. The 'Discurso', an anonymous manuscript, explains how in the pre-Inca period the first Indians timed their planting by the flowering of a particular cactus (a method which is still practised). Then, around A.D. 1400, the Inca Viracocha established a calendar based on twelve lunar months. Viracocha was succeeded by the Inca Pachacuti, the emperor said to be responsible for the *ceques*. When Pachacuti came to power, or so the story goes, he found the calendar to be in such a chaotic state that, on the advice of his council, he constructed certain sun towers or time-markers, known as *paca onancaq*, or probably the *sucancas* of the chroniclers. In principle, when the sun passed a certain sun tower it was time to sow early crops

147

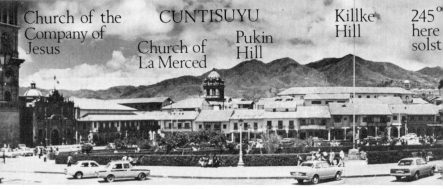

Church of the   CUNTISUYU   Killke   245°
Company of   Pukin   Hill   here
Jesus   Church of   Hill   solst
                 La Merced

The Plaza de Armas of Cuzco – the Huacaypata or Leisure Square of the Incas. Large stone-built markers were sited on the skyline to mark the position of the setting sun at the beginning of the year and the days for sowing crops.

(usually in August as we know it); when it was framed by two shorter towers it was time for the general sowing (usually September today).

Garcilaso recorded that he had seen the *sucancas* as a boy. He said there were four towers on each horizon – east and west – as seen from the Cuzco valley and that each group of four comprised two high towers and two lower ones. He also indicated their height: the lower towers were about three '*estados*', or roughly sixteen feet. Garcilaso mentions an apparent variation: large, carved 'pillars' sited in the temples, their shadows used by priests to nominate the dates of the equinoxes. Cobo mentions 'pillars' marking the months among his list of *ceques* and *wak'as* but his numbers vary and he makes no mention of height. As yet no one, not even Dr Chávez, has found any trace of the *sucancas*. He considers that as the *sucancas* were also *wak'as*, they would probably have been destroyed by the Spanish priests. Although I trusted his research, I felt I should look for them myself at some stage in my investigations.

When I asked Gerald Hawkins about the accuracy of such a system of towers, he said it would be of no use for establishing leap years and an exact solar calendar as we use today. It would be of more value in determining when or when not to insert intercalary months in a basically lunar calendar. It would be more like a Stonehenge system for finding, say, the first new moon after its summer solstice or even the observational type calendar of the pre-Islamic Arabs. With towers of this sort, the solstice could not be determined to closer than a few days. An equinox point, with the sun's displacement each day being greater, would be more exact. But here we would need to know where, if any, the sighting points were (it takes two points to make an alignment).

Although, obviously, the sun played a part in fixing certain times in the year, all the sources agreed that the lunar calendar continued as the basic festival calendar. The lunar months, which took their names from important festivals, were thought to be timed to begin with the 'new' moon and in January, or Kamay, for example, a fiesta was held on the day of the full moon, and a llama was sacrificed in the great square. Six days after that full moon the Indians 'took all the bones of the previous year's sacrifices and these they ground and mixed with coca, chili pepper, salt and burnt peanuts, flowers of many colours and *chicha*, the maize beer'. Finally this exotic sludge was poured into a river to be carried to the great creator god Viracocha.

The ceremonial calendar names December the Capac Raymi, or Magnificent Festival, in which 'boys of sixteen years' acquired the status of manhood and it seems to have marked the beginning of the Inca year. It was the first month of the heavy rainy season in the mountains and included the December solstice from which, in a way that is not fully understood, the Incas apparently counted the days and moons. With these facts in mind, I reckoned that finding the location and maybe some stones of one of the sun towers was worth trying. I felt that the easiest approach to this problem would be to use the elaborate photomosaic of the city of Cuzco which S.A.N. had prepared for me. By marking the angles of the solstices from the Plaza de Armas and drawing lines towards the 'horizon' I hoped to duplicate the techniques described by the anonymous author of the 'Discurso' who said specifically that the sun observations were made from the top of an *osno*, or observatory (probably a low mound), located in the main square of the city. Accordingly, I set out the plan in my hotel room, and having marked the solstice positions, I then had to locate the pillars on the ground. The area which bore most promise was the line to the western horizon at 295 degrees, or the point where I could expect the June solstice sunset. (To be completely accurate, the angular height of the horizon from the point of observation is necessary but unfortunately the height of the *osno* was not stated.)

In one part of his account Father Cobo had called the summer sun tower the 'Chirao-sucanca', and the winter tower 'Pucuy-sucanca'; elsewhere in his manuscript he describes the two pillars that marked the arrival of summer as the ninth *wak'a* on the sixth *ceque* of the Chinchasuyu or north-west quarter, on a hill known as Quiangalla on the road to the village of Yucay, a village to the north-west of Cuzco. He continues in the same passage to describe the seventh *wak'a* on the eighth *ceque* of the same quarter, which was known as '*sucanca*', as comprising two markers 'that indicated the time to sow maize by the arrival of the sun'.

I climbed the hill beside the cathedral and by following the list of *wak'as*, I gauged the places on the irregular skyline within a few hundred yards. The afternoon was just right for the venture and I set out purposefully along the old road to the Chinchasuyu through steep cobbled streets of the present district of Carmenga. I asked directions along the way, and half an hour later I reached the open hillside. Below me the city lay as a network of streets and squares; Ausangate, the snow-capped mountain, an *apu* or ancient lord, was directly beyond the end of the valley and partly hidden by towering white clouds.

Where had the sun towers been built? On the crest of the first hill, I reached a rocky outcrop that I had noticed from the *plaza*. The sun would set virtually behind it on 21 June. I searched between the rocks and found nothing, so I moved on and hunted north and south. Allowing for an angular error of plus or minus one degree in my bearing from the square (I had corrected for true north) I would have to search a little less than half a mile of the horizon. The going was hard and the climb took me over steep, uneven ground. Weathered rock and clumps of grass often momentarily raised my hopes but after five hours' hard walking, with the puzzle still unsolved, I too was convinced that the towers had been entirely destroyed, and that only excavation or thorough clearing of the ground would reveal anything.

My time had not been entirely wasted. One aspect of Inca astronomy at least referred me back to Nasca. There was no widely accepted reason for me to assume that the astronomical achievements of the

Nascas would have been any more sophisticated than that of the Incas. Now I felt I had stumbled upon a parallel that could be drawn between the two cultures, a parallel which somewhat paradoxically drew the theories for and against astronomy closer together.

The sun towers of Cuzco had emerged as an important aspect of the Inca calendar. They had been constructed in specific locations pinpointed by a simple day-count system probably calculated from a solstice. When the sun passed the sun towers the Indians knew the time had come for sowing, reaping or anything else. In addition the sun towers were *wak'as*, which gave the *wak'as* a certain astronomical significance. Few sun tower *wak'as*, however, were found on *ceques* and whether or not the *ceques* themselves had any astronomical purpose would remain an open question.

Taking the analogy to Nasca, I had seen a great number of piles of stones which in every way fitted the description of *wak'as*. If some had the same function as the sun towers, albeit in a more primitive form, there could be a case for assuming a simple calendar. So, in Nasca, stone heaps at the end of some lines, for example, could have been sited at places on the horizon marking a day 'sometime' after or before a solstice, using the same day-count basis that the Incas employed. Indeed the Nascas could simply have counted the days to 'the first full moon after a solstice', which would produce one moon solstice line. Each year there would be a different line. In a period of eighteen or nineteen years the lines would make a fan, or triangle. (The solstice moon reaches its extremes at declinations plus or minus twenty-nine degrees and plus or minus nineteen degrees every eighteen or nineteen years depending on a fifty-six year cycle.)

Certainly Maria Reiche had always spoken of 'lines' not 'stones' to mark the planting season or the time when water was expected in the rivers. Once she took me to a line near the large rectangle and said it 'marked the approach of a solstice', but then so could any line close to the limits of the extreme positions of the sun. As the computer had shown, without knowing the precise date of construction, some celestial object was at the end of every line at some date or other, yet few of them pointed to sun or moon *extrema*.

The imponderables of festival dates counted from the solstices had not been programmed by the Smithsonian team. Positive dates for the sites and for the festivals would have to be fed into the computer if this theory were to be proved. Such dates were unknown. Anyway, as Gerald Hawkins later reminded me, what of all those other lines outside the sixty-seven degrees east and west, where sun, moon and planets rise and set? What are they? These could not have been related to the solstices.

So if the answer did not lie in the heavens, it must lie on earth. Perhaps the remaining lines were random, leading to *wak'as* of other spiritual importance to the Indians. Or, alternatively, could the whole system of stone piles at Nasca have been a very simple counting device with perhaps one pile of stones for 'special days' between the solstices?

The idea that the *ceques* and *wak'as* of Cuzco could be a central part of the Inca calendar, either a recording device or incorporating a system of observation places and sun markers, was first put forward by Dr Tom Zuidema. An anthropology professor at the University of Illinois, Urbana, he began his investigations in Cuzco in 1954 when Dr Chávez helped him locate many of the shrines for a monumental analysis of the social organization of the Inca capital.

I flew to Urbana specially to meet Dr Zuidema, who maintained that several hypothetical calendars could be drawn up from looking at the arrangement of the shrines and lines. In his work he too was faced with the inconsistency of the chronicled accounts which never allowed one single sharply defined answer. As a result there was great variation in the number of sun towers and also in the tallies of the months. Most of the

The unique illustrated account of life in Inca times by Guamán Poma, lost for 300 years, was discovered in Copenhagen in 1908. One of the drawings gives some insight into the work of a *quipucamayoc* or '*quipu* keeper' and the abacus-like counting board used for calculations.

early writers agreed on a twelve-month lunar year but many of them failed to account for 'spare' days which must have accumulated, and the Inca names were often confused. Also Dr Zuidema had always to be mindful of the Spanish tendency to equate Inca months with Christian months.

Dr Zuidema formed four theories based on numbers. One of his calendars was derived from the following calculations. He gave each *ceque* a number value of either eight or ten, which according to different chroniclers were the totals of days in an Inca week. Then by assuming that the Cuntisuyu had nine *ceques* like the other three quarters in the quadripart division of Cuzco, one would arrive at a total of thirty-six *ceques*. By using a number value of ten this would yield a year of 360 days which bears comparison with details from at least one chronicler.

Zuidema drew my attention to another interesting aspect of the problem – the parallel between the arrangement of the shrines along the *ceques* and the knotted string Inca recording devices called *quipus* on which calendric information could have been recorded. A *quipu* generally consisted of a single cord to which a number of separate knotted strings were attached. Each string, each knot and the numbers of turns in each knot was a reminder of some information – possibly numbers,

harvest, census material, festivals, prayers, traditional stories and perhaps much else to be recorded by a people without a written language.
As a *quipu* was a memory aid the information was pertinent only to the
person who knotted the string, the specialist '*quipu* keeper' or *quipucamayoc*, and though possibly professional interpreters could understand
the meaning of the strings, no one today can decode the information.

Father Cobo said the strings of a *quipu* resembled those of a rosary
(possibly in some instances the purpose may have been similar). By
moving on to look at the numbers used by the Indians in their *quipus*
and religion, I found I had entered a very blurred zone. The precise
world of modern astronomy with its computers, calculations and *LED*
displays was ranged against an ever-increasing load of imponderables,
collectively and neatly described as the 'Indian mind'. Where to start, and
more especially what criteria to employ? On the one hand there was
solid evidence from authorities whose work was published and discussed; on the other, interpretation and speculation.

As early as 1947 Dr Kosok described some of the piles of smaller
stones at Nasca and suggested they could have been counting devices.
Maria Reiche had often told me the same. Their theories were based on
the chroniclers who recounted how stones and seeds were used on
boards with rows and compartments. The Indian chronicler Guaman
Poma de Ayala includes in his massive manuscript almost 400 pen and
ink illustrations of Indian life including one of a *quipucamayoc* with a
counting board alongside him.

The chronicles make it absolutely clear that calculations were made
with 'counters' and the results were recorded on *quipus*. A decimal
system of counting was involved: on one single *quipu* string tied to a

cord, the knot farthest away from the anchorage point represented single units. Two ties in a knot equalled two and so on. The next knot in line represented tens, and the next hundreds, then thousands. Ten thousand seems to have been the highest number ever encountered by modern *quipu* analysts. The system of counting was well suited to the Inca administration which was also organized in tens – at one extreme were foremen in charge of ten or fifty taxpayers ranging to the chief of 10,000 taxpayers. The system appears to allow for a zero which would be the space where a knot would be expected, though counting in tens does not necessarily show they had invented the zero. The concept ten, 'hundred', etc., contains ⋮ ⋮ ⋮ ⋮ ⋮ items. It does not imply a zero symbol. That was an Arab invention and greatly simplified arithmetic. The Romans have X, C, M. But they did not have a zero.

It occurred to me that a *ceque* might have linked all the information represented by the *wak'as* (or knots). A modern analogy would be a computer tape with all its information stored along its length. Here then was a numbers game *par excellence*, and a speculative one at that.

Father Cobo said that the *ceques* and *wak'as* of Cuzco were in the charge of a kinship group. Could the *wak'as* therefore have represented the number of families available to the Inca for tax purposes? I hesitate to suggest precisely how the *ceque* plan could be made into a huge tax assessment device. More plausible is a calendric purpose, with the *wak'as* representing days. But how would this have come about? Was it planned, or did the Indians simply create a special *wak'a* for each day as they counted from the solstice?

Quipus were essentially an Inca device (though today we still tie a knot in the end of our handkerchief), and were detailed by the chronic-

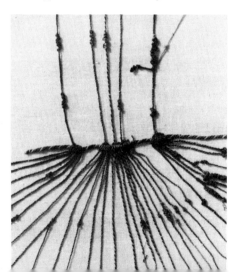

Quipus from graves on the Peruvian desert. (Courtesy of the Museo Regional de Ica, Peru.)

lers in their accounts of Inca life. The many *quipus* found near Ica and Nasca have come from Inca graves there. On the other hand, the coastal tribes could have had a similar device and some pottery designs with groups of patterns showing different numbers of drawings possibly represented '*quipu*-like' counting systems.

In Ica I learnt more about *quipus* when one afternoon Duncan Masson, the desert explorer, took me to the new local museum. The newness is relative to my first experience of the same collection which was once housed in an old building in the centre of the town; I had filmed there in 1963. The new museum now contains the finest collection of *quipus* in Peru, and Duncan introduced me to Dr Alejandro Pezzia, the director and his long-time friend who offered to show them all to us.

'Each of these represents something – the secret died with the man,' he explained, pointing to large frames covered with coarse muslin. The *quipus* had been spread over them so that the individual strings were clearly displayed. They held me like a *trompe l'oeil*, the product of a peculiar art that has strange dimensions. What was the secret of these fragile strings?

'Look at these.'

The cords were protected under thin translucent plastic film. Dr Pezzia indicated two cords, one brown, one pale orange. Another slightly thicker cord had been twisted from two coloured strings.

'These must have meant something – it would be wonderful to know what.'

I moved for a moment across the cool, sunshaded room. Duncan and Dr Pezzia provided the cues: 'Harvest, population, even the number of pots made by a craftsman – all the history of a village or family unit could be tied in these knots. If only we could use them to look back through time.' My mind returned to the lines. Supposing each line at Nasca had been owned by a family for a reason, perhaps simply for the *wak'a* at the end of the line. The piles of stones could represent the number of people in a family and the number of offerings made to the *wak'a*; or each stone, by virtue of its place on the line, could have represented a day between fiestas as in a simple calendar.

Duncan Masson had already expressed his opinion: the piles of stones in the clearings could quite simply be heaps made in the process of construction. Dr Pezzia had no particular theory: he would listen to them all and then make an assessment.

Dr Pezzia had carefully removed the cover from the exhibit and I saw the detail perfectly. One six-inch-long cord acted as anchorage for two main divisions of knotted strings. I chose the smaller set for a simple exercise. Five strings had been tied to the cord: one at each end, and three nearer the centre. The totals were easy to deduce by counting the knots and following the agreed formula. String one amounted to 5,530 and string two totalled 470. Without a single clue to their meaning, it would have been fruitless to continue, apart from one interesting feature. Many knots represented seven. Seven had obviously been an important number to people 500 years ago. What had they been counting?

One bid to decipher *quipus* had also revealed totals of seven and numbers divisible by seven. Erland Nordenskiöld was born in 1877 in Ström, north of Stockholm, of a family of explorers. Young Erland began exploring South America at the age of twenty-two. His studies led him into anthropology and the various native cultures and eventually to the *quipus*. He noticed the recurring seven and so developed an idea that it was a sacred number. Why seven? He published his work in 1925 in the period when experimental psychologists were investigating man's subconscious and creating startling new theories. Had he been influenced by the work in Europe? Not everyone agrees with Nordenskiöld's conclusions, although numerologists, who study the sacred numbers of religion and mythology, have noticed the apparent preference of the human mind for certain numbers, especially seven. There are, for instance, seven deadly sins and seven days in a week. The Book of Proverbs in the Bible mentions seven pillars of wisdom and, of course, there are the seven wonders of the world. The prevalence of the 'mystic' seven has been ascribed to the numbers of stars in certain constellations, such as the seven brightest stars of the Great Bear – Ursa Major. Perhaps with more relevance to the Indians of coastal Peru, the Pleiades were so called after the 'seven sisters', the daughters of Atlas and Pleione of Greek mythology.

Erland Nordenskiöld also suggested that *quipus* contained information about the rotation periods of various celestial bodies, and he supported the theory by calculations made from the numbers on the knots. It implied the Indians had more astronomical knowledge than other evidence suggests and it awaits proof.

Quipus aside, the number seven does not seem to have been especially important to the Incas, or at least the chroniclers were silent about it. Three, however, was undoubtedly the favoured number – a child to be sacrificed walked three times around the *wak'a*; three of the quarters or *suyus* of Cuzco held three groups of three *ceques*. Each group of three *ceques* repeated three names: 'Collana' (meaning 'excellent'), 'Payan' and 'Cayao' – names without a clear translation. Each represented a kinship group – Collana being the highest order. The odd man out was the south-west quarter or Cuntisuyu which had either fourteen or fifteen *ceques* and some irregularity in the names. (The Cobo manuscript says the eighth *ceque* was named Callao for the first half and Collana for the second half.) If the total number of *ceques* in the quarter is counted by names, the number reached is fifteen which, of course, *is* divisible by three.

These triplets of *ceques* were arranged in a strange way which was deduced by Dr Zuidema with the help of Chávez Ballón. Using the names listed by Father Cobo, and plotting these against known *wak'a* positions, Dr Zuidema arrived at a plan in which the sequences of the *ceques* in the northern half are clockwise, always from the east: Collana, Payan, Cayao. In the southern half it was anti-clockwise. Why? Perhaps it might have some correspondence with the revolution of the celestial sphere.

Curiously, three was not only emphasized by the arrangement of the *ceques*; an analysis of Father Cobo's list of the individual shrines also reveals how three stones were often the object of veneration. The ninth shrine of the fifth *ceque* of Antisuyu was 'three stones on a hill'; the fifth shrine of the eighth *ceque* of the same quarter was 'three stones', and in Collasuyu the sixth shrine of the second *ceque* was 'three stones near a village'. Altogether eleven shrines included 'three'. The next most favoured number was five. Ten was mentioned four times and only in the Cuntisuyu. Two was the only other number specified – it appeared just once in the Collasuyu as 'two stones near the settlement of Quijalla where offerings of small shells and burnt cloth were made'.

By the end of my stay in Cuzco, I had seen more numbers squeezed out of *ceques* and *wak'as* than from all my daily travel balance sheets put together. I had clearly exhausted this field of material, for the moment at least. It now remained for me to pursue my research into the Indian mind. Who were the spirits venerated at the *wak'as*? I would try another approach and observe firsthand the surviving religious customs of the Indian peoples.

7   Pathways in the Andes

Offerings are made at a shrine in the Andes.

The gods and spirits of ancient Peru were manifold and the creator was the greatest of all. For the Incas, he represented a man, Viracocha, and in Cuzco they sculpted an image of him in solid gold, the size of a ten-year-old boy, his right arm raised in command. For the Spanish priests, Viracocha and the galaxy of lesser gods represented paganism, to be ruthlessly eradicated from the Indian peoples they had conquered. Their efforts, as fanatical and thorough as any known in history, were largely successful, on the surface at least. Clerics produced countless reports on almost every facet of Indian religious custom and, armed

Young girls of outstanding beauty and physical perfection were chosen in every village of the Inca Empire. The *aclla-conas* or 'chosen women' were educated by the Government in special convents or *acllahuasi* and were under the care of the *mamacunas* or 'mothers'. The girls were taught religion and their practical chores included the preparation of *chicha* – maize beer – for sacrificial rites.

with this knowledge, they were instructed to destroy, cleanse and convert.

Many chronicles concerned the religion of the Incas. Less was written about the other peoples of ancient Pirú, especially of the tribes of the coastal valleys, before the Incas established their religious influence there. Father Calancha wrote of moon worship on the north coast and of the importance of the Pleiades. Other sources mentioned Pachacámac, a coastal equivalent of Viracocha, together with mythological beings and animal divinities, particularly peculiar feline-like images, serpents and condors.

The exact sequence of the development of the religion among the ancient peoples has been, like the astronomy, the subject of much speculation. All the sources seem to agree, though, that the Indians venerated high places, the sky and the earth and many natural things around them. The practice of ancestor worship was also universal and the elaborate burials of the coast people imply a parallel with the well-documented ancestor worship of the Incas. Polo de Ondegardo was successful in finding three mummies of Inca emperors and two of empresses: they had been enclosed in some form of copper cage. Polo destroyed them. Another report on Cuzco's Temple of the Sun vividly described how two royal mummies were kept within a sanctuary where 'an old lady wearing a golden mask fanned the flies away'.

That story took on an unexpected significance when I visited a small Peruvian village deep in the mountains for the annual festival of Corpus Christi. Hundreds of Indians had gathered in the main square, all wearing their finest clothes: a moving wave of faces between deep red ponchos of hand-spun wool. Whitewashed walls of adobe mud-brick houses stood on every side, their flimsy-looking balconies weighed down with more spectators. The door of the tiny church was flung open and a soft, sweet smell of incense hung in the air.

The crowd moved in two streams, entering and leaving the church. I found myself carried as on a tide into the dark interior where a smoky gloom was pierced by sharp rays of sunlight from an opening high in the roof. In an alcove set apart on the south side, a group of Indians were playing sad, reedy notes on ancient flutes. I peered into the gloom and watched fascinated as an old lady bent over a small earthen bowl: she was heating it on a tiny brazier filled with lighted sticks, as if quite unaware of the clamour around her and the watching Indians. A pungent steam replaced the incense smell.

'What's happening?' I whispered to one of the Indians in Spanish.

He looked towards the woman and turned to me shyly. 'She's a *mamacuna* – one of the old ones.'

I nodded thanks, understanding at last, and turned and followed the slowly moving crowd outside. *Mamacuna* was the Inca name for certain consecrated women – the Chosen Women – who taught religion to selected virgins or *acllas*, training them in the practical preparation of fine *chicha* (maize beer) for sacrifices or offerings to the *wak'as*. Here was my first living connection with a *wak'a*.

How many other *wak'as* could I find in use today and where? One type I had seen already. The *apacita* is usually set on roads at mountain passes or other places of danger. Anyone passing along the road makes an offering, usually a stone, perhaps some coca or items from his or her person, such as old sandals. Gradually the pile is augmented and in places the stone heaps are now enormous.

An *apacita* at a snowy Andean pass.

Other *wak'as* are the home of the wind or the sources of the all too frequent earthquakes. Or rainbows. The chronicler Sarmiento related this particular god to the hill of Huanacauri outside Cuzco. But, scientifically, rainbows are a strange phenomenon: if one Indian had built a *wak'a* at the spot he had seen as the end of a rainbow, another Indian standing only a few hundred yards away would see the rainbow in a different position and have to site his shrine in a completely different place.

It was the seemingly random aspect of the Indians' spiritual beliefs that intrigued me; an aspect which made space for the personal belief of the individual. How did it work though, in practice? What was the connection between the *wak'as*, the *ceques* and the lines? I would pursue other living evidence of Indian religious belief.

Ironically, the next step had been decided for me about ten years previously, when, with Marion, I had been filming rare flamingos in a remote part of the Andes. At the top of a hill I found a sacrifice, a hearth with ashes and calcined llama bones. The hill overlooked a lake covered with pink birds and, in the opposite direction, a cold empty plain that stretched endlessly to the horizon. Leading from the hill to the plain, a line led as straight as an arrow beneath a cloudless sky. It was a remote area, sparsely inhabited, and criss-crossed by many paths very similar to those in Nasca; and the sacrifice paralleled those offered to the *wak'as* of Cuzco. The line I saw in 1967 was then in use, of that I was certain. But had the tradition died out in the intervening years?

I spent many months in Nasca and Cuzco gathering information, and at last I was ready to make another journey south, into these high, desolate *cordilleras*, as the mountain ranges are known, of the Bolivian Andes. Armed with carefully prepared questions, I began to organize an expedition which would lead from Cuzco to La Paz, the Bolivian capital, and then a long way further south to the people who had made the sacrifice and who, I hoped, would reveal the significance of the lines, *wak'as* and *ceques*. En route I would take in Puno, Lake Titicaca and Tiwanaku, a site famous for extensive pre-Inca ruins set in the ancient land of Collao.

In the sixteenth century Collao was the largest and most populated province of the wealthy viceroyalty of Peru: its name was probably a Spanish corruption of the Inca word '*Colla*', used to describe the Aymara Indian people who inhabited the southern part of their great empire. More specifically, the Collas were an Aymara sub-tribe with a separate state near the present town of Puno, my first stop.

A road and a railway track run virtually together for most of the 240 miles from Cuzco to Puno, offering a choice of somewhat dubious comforts for the long journey through the mountains. Although the bus services have improved a thousandfold since I first made the trip, and now boast air-conditioning, bars and stewardesses, it was still a dirt road and my choice remained firmly with the train. The line is part of South American history and an unforgettable experience for any railway enthusiast. Also in its favour was the reported state of the road over the mountains: the rains had only just finished and truck drivers told horrific stories of deep snow on one high pass.

The railway track, brilliantly engineered by American Henry Meiggs, took twenty-five years to build. It was completed in 1907 and as a single line it painfully climbs out of one valley over a 14,153 foot pass at La Raya (higher than Pikes Peak, Colorado, by forty-three feet), and then descends into a totally different region of the Andes, a high, cold plateau known as the *altiplano*. Along the way, a panorama of tiny Indian villages and patchwork fields unfolds. The pace is leisurely: there is time to take photographs, chat to local spectators, barter in busy trackside markets or even collect wild flowers.

Twelve hours after leaving Cuzco the lofty orange and beige coaches are shunted on to a quay in the small but crowded lake-port of Puno, where passengers bound for Bolivia transfer to a steamer – on this occasion the S.S. *Inca*, only 650 tons. This is the highlight of the journey. The vintage ship – it was built in Britain in 1905 – was taken up to Puno in pieces and assembled on the shore of the lake. Overnight it ploughs smoothly across the clear surface at 12,497 feet, the highest navigable water in the world. The lake, 110 miles by thirty-five, is in effect suspended between mountains, over two miles above the Pacific, and I have always remembered it as a most spectacular landmark.

Once, about 15,000 years ago near the end of the last ice age, it was part of a much larger system of lakes which lay between the same Andean *cordilleras*. Signs of these ancient lakes are abundant: the old beach levels remain like scars on the hillside in some places, and north and south of the present lake huge areas of flat *altiplano* are permanent reminders of the later drying stages. These vast open spaces, scoured almost bare by cold winds, have their greatest area south of Lake Titicaca. There, 250 miles south, one particularly inhospitable region has been the focus of many of my previous expeditions. It was my destination now.

I made a circuit of the deck as we steamed out of Puno. The air temperature must have been close to freezing: it was too cold for relaxing on the deck, leaning on the rail and watching the dark water. As the lights of Puno receded astern, the black Andean sky ahead filled with brilliant stars. There would be no visibility problems for native astronomers in this part of the mountains – at least not in the dryer,

164

Fifteen thousand years ago an immense lake covered the land between the *cordilleras* of the central Andes.

colder months – that is if they did not die of exposure first. I shivered and went below to a narrow bunk in a cabin shared with two hardy Swiss mountaineers.

The breakfast bell is rung on the ship at either six or seven depending on whether the crew has remembered the time change at the frontier which virtually bisects Lake Titicaca. Dawn reveals the narrowest section of the lake, the Straits of Tiquina on the Bolivian side. On the east, massive snow-capped mountains rise from the lake shore to peaks above 21,000 feet high. The west is not so rugged, though high ranges more than a hundred miles away form the final barrier above the Pacific.

I always feel at home in Bolivia, and since 1961 my travels have taken me to almost every part of the country. The geography is breathtaking: the mountains are in the record-breaking league, with Ancohuma at over 22,500 feet vying with Aconcagua in Argentina for the honour of being America's highest. To the east of the Andes dense forests fringe the Amazon and, although Bolivia has been landlocked since the 'Nitrate War' with Chile in 1879, immense and wildly desolate high altitude deserts present the same barren aspect as the stony *pampas* of coastal Peru. As a zoologist and photographer, I know these habitats deserve special attention, and Marion and I have penetrated many of their remote areas with Bolivian companions who have become long-standing friends. We have been through a good many nightmares together.

Now, as the steamer approached land, the sky reflected pale blue from the mirror-like surface of the lake, flawed by a solitary cloud. The image was disturbed only by a pair of coppery grebes which dived as we glided past. Ten minutes more and the S.S. *Inca* would dock at Guaqui, Bolivia's main lake-port. Marion was to meet me at the dockside with a jeep in which to make the fifty-mile road journey to La Paz, where she had spent the past week arranging meetings with local experts.

The *aduanero* (customs man) was quick and efficient: within ten minutes of landing, my bags were cleared and we drove the jeep out of the docks.

'First stop is the *transito*.' Marion searched the glove box for the special pass issued for all road journeys in Bolivia: it includes a small toll per mile. The *transito* officer, dressed in dark blue and incongruously smart for the dusty Andean winter, approached the jeep and examined the paper. Then with a nod and a cheery wave, he said '*Sigue no mas, señora.*' No problems.

Before Marion had time to let in the clutch, a group of Aymara men and women, all in their best clothes, frantically signalled us to stop. A round-faced girl aged about seventeen spoke in Spanish, '*Señora, por favor*' . . . She explained that they had missed the bus to Tiwanaku and asked if we could give them a lift.

Marion looked at me. Tiwanaku, the next village, was only eleven miles and we planned to stop there anyway.

'All ten?' I asked in Spanish.

The Aymara girl's expression brightened, her bronze cheeks contrasting with a broad grin that revealed a remarkably fine set of sturdy teeth, '*Señor*,' and once again an explanation. 'Her cousin – there's a wedding – they were late.'

I winced at the thought of ten of them piling in: we had a large jeep station wagon, but we were already well loaded. Eventually we reached a compromise figure of six. Speaking rapidly among themselves in Aymara, they selected the six we would take.

Marion opened the side door and two men in brown suits and dark fedora hats, and four women in brightly coloured satin skirts, or *polleras*, climbed in.

'*Buenos, buenos días*,' everyone chorused.

The young girl wore a colourfully striped blanket or *aguayo* over her shoulder. A sudden movement inside the blanket was followed by a series of high-pitched squeaks. An older woman laughed when I asked about the baby.

'*No es wa'wa, – es chanchito*,' she said, 'not a baby, it's a piglet – a present for the bride!'

We chatted and I showed them a picture of our small daughter.

'*Que bonita*' – 'How pretty!' They crowded around to get a better view. 'What a large baby! How old? *Inglesa*?' They had learnt in school that England was somewhere far away.

The Aymara of the *altiplano* are a stocky people. Their name seems to have been introduced by Polo de Ondegardo in 1559; before then they were apparently known as the *Haque*, meaning 'humans'. Less than 500 years ago they were divided into separate tribes occupying a territory which extended from north of the pass of La Raya, in Peru, to the Andean *cordilleras* east and west of Lake Titicaca, and south through much of the *altiplano* in present-day Bolivia.

Around the northern part of Lake Titicaca, two of the tribes, the Lupacas and Collas, were traditional enemies, and as the Inca armies moved into the Collasuyu in the years between 1430 and 1493, the Aymara-speaking tribes were subjugated with varying degrees of success. It was one of the least stable parts of the Inca Empire and even after the Spanish finally completed their conquest of the area in 1542, local uprisings frequently occurred. Thus, by tradition and history, the Aymara have been described as aggressive, stolid and uninspired: the result of a history of repression, and the wild nature of their homeland. Not that the lakeside looked inhospitable this June: the sky was a vivid blue, and along the road, as more people converged on Tiwanaku, we passed the occasional patch of brilliant chemical colour, provided by German pharmaceuticals, of the gaudy festival dresses.

Marion drove into the village square and parked in front of a large green-painted bandstand, roofed with corrugated iron. 'Home from home,' she smiled as we helped bundle the last woman and the piglet, now protesting loudly, out of the jeep. She had first come to Bolivia in

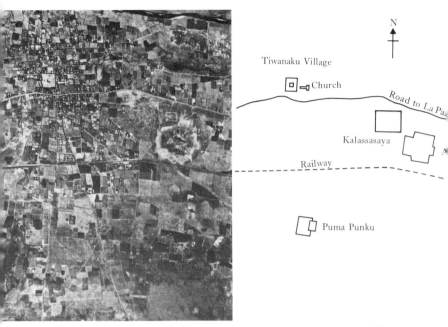

The site of Tiwanaku covered almost two square miles when it was completed. The most prominent construction was the stepped pyramid – Akapana – which today is roughly fifty feet high. A raised platform faced with dressed stone – the Kalassasaya – stands to the north-west, and a similar terreplein, the Puma Punku, lies 984 yards to the south-west.

1962 to work with an Aymara community on the lakeside and Tiwanaku had been her nearest 'shopping centre'.

Tiwanaku is a very ancient settlement and famous for the pre-Inca ruins that lie less than a mile to the south-east of the village. We had come to talk with Carlos Ponce Sanginés, the Director of the Tiwanaku Investigation Centre. Carlos Ponce has been studying the archaeology of the site for more than a quarter of a century, and since the 1950s has been conducting a massive excavation and reconstruction project. He greeted us at the recently completed 'site HQ'. Marion had met him in La Paz to discuss my interest in the history, the possible astronomical alignments, and the dualistic social divisions which apparently existed in Tiwanaku, and were similar to those of ancient Cuzco. Also Carlos Ponce had said that old settlements lay north and south of the ruins in a straight line, yet were not visible from each other.

We shook hands. '*Buenos días, señora,*' Carlos Ponce greeted us, then asked about our journey. I explained our stop and delay along the way as we crossed the road to the site. He led the way to the ruins, now surrounded by a high wire fence. 'So much damage has been done in the past,' he explained, 'that the site now has to be protected.' Many of the stones, he said, had been dismantled and re-used by the Spanish as foundation for the present village: some of the perfectly hand-shaped stones are visible in the church, others even reached as far as La Paz, where they were used in a mill for grinding cocoa.

Ancient Tiwanaku stands on a flat plain only ninety-eight feet above the level of the lake, against a background of low red sandstone hills. We followed a narrow path worn between clumps of yellowing puna grass, their long needle-like leaves hard and tough, shaped to reduce water loss in the cold dry season.

Carlos Ponce explained that the site covered four square kilometres. The principal features were a low stone-faced platform, the Kalassas-aya, now reconstructed and standing close to the main road to La Paz; a stepped pyramid, the Akapana, only a few yards to the south-east; two other smaller groups of ruins in the same sector; and the Puma Punku, another platform, which stands isolated from the main ruins more than half a mile to the south-west. Here, as old pictures show, some of the most impressive stonework has been scattered on the ground for at least a century.

When the nineteenth-century travellers described it, the whole of Tiwanaku had collapsed. Legend and mystery quickly grew around the ruins. One writer suggested that Tiwanaku was the 'cradle of American man', a statement which was later embellished to 'the centre of world civilization'. More dramatic stories described a massive flood – even a world-encircling tidal wave – and extraordinary changes in the earth's rotation period. Some of the features of Tiwanaku, at first sight, bear this out: the ruins *are* covered by a heavy layer of soil and even some of the higher structures are buried by layers of earth six feet deep. In parts, stones, some of them weighing over 100 tons, are scattered as if tossed about by a giant's hand.

What is probably the first pictorial representation was made by a French explorer, Alcide D'Orbigny, who visited Tiwanaku in 1833. He sketched a row of stones in front of the earthen hill of the Akapana, itself depicted with stone blocks littering the sloping side, like dominoes thrown on a carpet. On the same sketch a man is working two bullocks and a plough over the site of even more ruins. By 1896 an early photograph showed little change, and when I first visited the site in 1961, the earth cover of the Kalassasaya was then being removed in the early stages of the latest series of excavations.

The Bolivian Tiwanaku Research Centre headed by Carlos Ponce has now produced a carefully documented history of these impressive ruins. Far from being the work of extraterrestrials, they were the work of ancestors of the Aymara who first settled near Lake Titicaca, probably around 1580 B.C., and established themselves as simple farmers. Archaeological evidence suggests that they led rather unspectacular lives until, in approximately the first century A.D., something happened to set the people on the road to greatness: perhaps a gradual change of climate favoured better food production. This change stimulated the development of political and social organization, at least to a level high enough to organize the design, labour and construction of large buildings. Much of the red sandstone was quarried from a formation in the *altiplano* (the nearest source is only five miles away), but andesite for the large gateways with their intricately sculpted decorations probably came from a peninsula in the lake. Basalts for some of the finely worked statues originated from volcanic hills 170 miles away in the southern *altiplano*.

Some of the stone blocks used in the Puma Punku were truly massive and bear comparison with the size of the shaped stones used at Stonehenge. The largest single block of the Puma Punku is of sand-

Large upright stones show the line of the Kalassasaya covered by a ploughed field in 1896. The village of Tiwanaku is on the left. Excavation and reconstruction in the late 1960s (bottom left) have exposed the platform of Kalassasaya and a sunken 'temple'.

stone over twenty-five feet long with a volume exceeding 1,500 cubic feet and weighing between 100 and 131 tons. If this stone came from the nearest sandstone quarry it represents a massive expenditure of human energy. The largest stones of Stonehenge are thirty tons and were moved twenty miles which Gerald Hawkins calculated would have taken 700 men twenty days per stone. The smaller 'bluestones' of Stonehenge came from a distant source and average four tons each. They were transported 240 miles (including 215 miles by water). Similarly some of the Puma Punku andesite stones had to be moved thirty-seven miles, which if taken the shortest way would have included a journey across part of Lake Titicaca. The largest of these stones, listed as 'block 10', is more than 11½ feet long, and with a volume of 237 cubic feet is estimated to weigh over sixteen tons. Not only did these massive stones have to be quarried and transported; they were carefully dressed and moved into precise positions as homage to ancient Aymara gods.

The Gods

Myths trace the origin of the Aymara people to Tiwanaku and their legends
of gods and spirits have many variations. They say: 'The creator Viracocha
rose from Lake Titicaca in a time of primitive darkness – other gods exist in
mountains and rivers – in the thunder and lightning. Wicked men were
turned to stone and spirits belong to caves and springs.' Tiwanaku was
deserted by the time the Spanish arrived and the history was already
confused, so the monolithic figures may never be identified.

In the relatively short period of 500 years the importance of Tiwanaku grew. The people produced a massive ceremonial centre which, Carlos Ponce suggests, was built in the eight months of each year when they could leave their fields. Apparently there is no evidence to suggest any form of slave labour – the people created the edifices as a mark of respect to their gods. Images in the form of huge monolithic statues and finely carved friezes show these gods with large doleful faces and empty eyes, and the many geometric patterns give some precious insight into the ancient Andean mind.

Juan de Betánzos, one of the earliest Spanish writers, whose *Suma y narración de los Incas* was prepared in 1551 for the second viceroy of Peru, Don Antonio de Mendoza, gives possibly the most informative account of the origin myth of the Collas – the people of the area.

'They [the Collas] tell of how in ancient times the land was dark, it was without light or day. In those times there lived a people who owed allegiance to an overlord whose name they no longer remember. In those days of darkness there came forth from a lake in the district of Collasuyu a lord named Con Ticci Viracocha, bringing with him a certain number of people, though they do not know how many. After emerging from the lake he went to a place nearby, they call it Tiaguanacu. While he was there, he suddenly made the sun and the day and commanded the sun to follow the course it does follow.'

Then he made the stars and the moon. According to the same legend, Con Ticci Viracocha had risen from the lake once before and 'he had made heaven and earth and left everything dark'.

It was this legend that set the Norwegian Thor Heyerdahl on his Kon Tiki raft expedition across the Pacific in 1947 in an attempt to follow a further strand of the legend. Viracocha had apparently set off from the Collao towards Cuzco and thence in the direction of the Pacific coast where, as Betánzos recorded, 'joined by his followers he put to sea in their company – they say he and his people went by water as easily as they traversed the land'.

'The name – Tiwanaku – when was it first used?' Marion asked.

Carlos Ponce referred her to the chronicles. The legend came from Inca times, and was recorded by the indefatigable Father Cobo, who says the earliest references are to Taypicala, an Aymara word that meant 'stone in the middle', because the Indians of Collao believed the place was in the middle of the world. Then, according to Father Cobo, who travelled in the Collasuyu between 1615 and 1618, the name was changed to Tiaguanaco, and he relates a delightful story: 'While the

Excavations in 1977 at the base of the Akapana.

Incas occupied the site and used the temple, a messenger arrived from Cuzco in such an extraordinarily short time that the Inca who knew how quickly he had come said to him, "Tiay guanacu", which in his language meant "Sit and rest, guanaco".' The guanaco is the wild, fleet-footed relative of the Andean llama. And so, said Cobo, 'the Inca, having given him this name, it remained with the people and since that time the place has been called Tiaguanaco'. From which we get the form Tiahuanaco and, more recently, Tiwanaku.

Cobo's seventeenth-century description of Tiwanaku implies that the buildings were not completely ruined at that time, though he admits that 'no one, not even a trustworthy informant, knew when they had been built'. It seems clear that they had been abandoned, uncompleted, before the Inca advanced into the area, probably because of strife among the Aymara tribes. Father Cobo continues: 'However all seem to agree that the buildings were very old, that they had been built long before the Incas – indeed the Incas modelled their grand buildings in

Cuzco on them – and some even suggested that Tiwanaku was built before the flood, and that it was some big building erected by giants.' Not that many modern historians would agree with Father Cobo, especially with his references to the stonework as a model for Cuzco. No pottery of the Tiwanaku design and age is known from the site of Cuzco.

We stopped at the base of the pyramid of Akapana. It had the rounded appearance of the hill in D'Orbigny's nineteenth-century engraving but it is now clearly identifiable as a pyramid – the result of Carlos Ponce's latest excavations. These have exposed at least three levels, constructed of walls retaining the original earthen mound, probably a natural hill.

I was helped into a five-foot deep pit on the eastern side of the pyramid where Bolivian archaeologists were carefully cleaning the earth from a freshly uncovered stone wall. The style was typical of Tiwanaku. Sandstone uprights, the height of a man, stood with rows of well-smoothed smaller stones laid between. Carlos Ponce explained that the smooth surfaces and accurate edges of the block-like stones had been produced by laborious rubbing, though the sandstone was a a relatively soft rock.

But why the covering of earth? Even the top of the pyramid had a layer as much as five feet deep and the earth, now compacted, must have covered the pyramid for centuries. Where did it come from? The most likely explanation is that, in common with other Andean structures, the sturdily built stone foundations were surmounted by equally well-made adobe mud structures. In the case of the Akapana, these could have been both for ceremonial and defensive purposes. But once the pyramid had been deserted, successive rainy seasons would reduce the adobe to a fine mud coating.

I asked Carlos Ponce if he believed the pyramid was aligned in any particular direction. 'North, south, east, west,' he replied without hesitation. 'But the accuracy will only be determined once the foundations are fully exposed.'

I made a rough check with a pocket compass. The alignments seemed to fit within about three degrees.

Father Cobo's narrative mentioned the Akapana as 'four or five *estados* [over twenty feet] in height, like a small hill, with large stone foundations'. So they had been exposed in his time? Perhaps. He continues: 'It is square and every so often has crossbeams or round turrets as of a fort.' The crossbeams have gone, so have the turrets. Perhaps they were

A depression at the top of the Akapana opens to the east. The construction is stone-lined and filled with water in the rainy season.

royal tombs or round burial towers known as *chullpas*, some of which remain standing in the central Andes today.

Getting to the top of the mound is easy, as tourists have left a well-worn path. On the eastern half of the upper part of the pyramid, a deep depression holds water after the rains. Sometimes it is referred to as a reservoir, and it is partly stone-lined, yet I suspected it had another purpose. Treasure seekers at some time in the past might have been responsible for tearing away the many tons of earth and Carlos Ponce pointed to a heap nearby. But it was the orientation of the depression that most interested me. Eastwards. Later I was able to compare it with similar features of pyramids on the Peruvian coast – an aerial view of the Kahuachi pyramid at Nasca shows a depression oriented in the same easterly direction. Like the Inca, the Aymara are known to face east for certain ceremonies: sunrise is particularly important and, according to one anthropologist, all offerings were made facing the rising sun.

Another excavation was in progress at the separate Puma Punku mound. The name, Cobo tells us, means 'Gate of the Lion', lion being the European approximation to the South American puma. The priest described Puma Punku as 'a flat-topped hillock made by hand, with a height of two *estados* [roughly ten feet] founded on large, well-worked stones which are shaped like the slabs we put on our tombs'.

When, in the nineteenth century, the first European explorers were allowed into South America, they sketched these huge carefully worked slabs of stone, the main characteristic of the Puma Punku, strewn across the ground with apparent disregard for their size. A plausible explanation for the chaos was offered by Cobo, years earlier: Spanish treasure seekers for whom 'in truth, this greed to possess the treasures which common belief supposes to be hidden there' had been a chief cause of the despoliation of the site.

I asked Carlos Ponce if his team had uncovered gold or silver.

'Nothing much in Tiwanaku so far.' It was a slightly rueful reply, so I ventured: 'How about spaceships?' He grinned at my allusion to the latest theories for the megaliths, then laughed.

'Absolutely none of those either!'

Marion was kneeling to photograph a detail on fallen stone. It had been part of a small gateway, two sides and an arch, all shaped from a

Ancient craftsmen drilled the tiny holes in this hard andesite rock.

An excavation in 1977 exposes the fine worked stones of the Puma Punku platform.

solid piece of andesite and intricately carved in a frieze across the arch.

'Look at this,' she called. Her camera was pointed at minute holes that at some time had been neatly drilled into strategic parts of the design. I knelt down to get a better look. The holes, each no more than three or four millimetres in diameter, could have been drilled by the original sculptors, using spun sticks and a grinding paste of harder rock. This archway and the holes have been well described by Carlos Ponce who suggests that very probably they held the supports of a metal sheet surrounding the carved figures.

When we reached the south side of the Puma Punku 'Gate of the Lion' mound, Carlos Ponce introduced me to his site director, Gregorio Cordero, a cheerfully energetic man, also well known throughout the world of Andean archaeology. He walked with us along the edge of an open pit from which 150 cubic yards of earth had already been removed. A perfect edge of a stone platform was exposed, each block fitting as neatly as cut lumps in a box of sugar. A trial trench had been dug into the mound from the south, revealing even more walls. The platform beneath would be absolutely perfect and the mud, far from being a disaster, had provided centuries-long protection from erosion by the weather.

Carlos Ponce and Señor Cordero called to me. They were ready. The Institute's surveyor, Ingeniero Waldo Parra, had set up his theodolite and fixed a simple baseline. This was the moment I had been waiting for. How was the Puma Punku mound aligned? This time it was not to be a crude measurement taken on a line roughly conforming to the shape of the earthen cover. Carlos Ponce's work had now exposed an edge as straight as the surveyor's line could be drawn. For the first time an accurate check could be made.

'Move to your left.' The call was made to a workman to move his ranging pole close to the line.

'*Bueno* – fine, now hold it steady – don't move.'

Ingeniero Parra took a reading and then checked his base-line – 95 degrees magnetic. He could not check the reading over more than twenty yards of exposed wall, as that was the full extent of the trial excavation. So the theodolite was moved along the mound and ranging poles set up in line with a measure drawn firmly tight to give an approximate extension of the straight edge of the exposed masonry. Again the same result but closer to east: 93° 16′. My compass gave 94 degrees. Allowing for the difference between true north and magnetic north, the line was three degrees south of east. This was not an accurate alignment to due east. What was the reason for the skew?

When the surveyor had finished at Puma Punku, we walked back to the Kalassasaya, Marion stopping on the way at the site museum to photograph some bowls and shallow vessels in brown ceramic, decorated with brown and red geometric designs. These were typical of Tiwanaku and had been found during earlier excavations.

At the reconstructed platform Ingeniero Parra took an azimuth along one side, a distance of 420 feet. Exactly two degrees off the due east–west line – corrected to the local difference between true and magnetic north, it would have been out by only a degree.

'All of them seem to have been east–west,' I said while the surveyor made a note in his book. As he wrote, my mind was searching for a point I had noticed and only visually recorded. What was it? I should have made a sketch. Kalassasaya, Akapana, high adobe structure on top, the horizon – that was the difference. Why had the Puma Punku been set at some distance from the main structures? There was something different about the Puma Punku. I raced back through the spiky grass, waving hurriedly to Marion on the way.

Breathless from running in the thin air, I sat on one of the massive slabs of smooth andesite on the top of the Puma Punku. The horizon to

The narrow gully or Quebrada Kirisa forms a low point in the horizon. Mount Illimani stands fifty-eight miles to the east of the ruins and appears above the *quebrada* only when viewed from the Puma Punku. At the equinox in March and September the sun rises slightly to the left (north) of the mountain.

the east – that was the difference. From Puma Punku, there was a direct, unobscured line eastwards to triple-peaked Illimani, a 21,000-foot snow-covered mountain, and if the angles we had just taken were correct, the sun would rise over the left shoulder of Illimani or slightly to the north of the peak on the equinox dates, 21 March and 23 September. The same mountain is virtually obscured from the Akapana and the Kalassasaya at ground level, hidden by hills 850 feet high. It is the only mountain visible on the eastern horizon, as it stands beyond a low pass through the hills.

As Carlos Ponce pointed out, the Puma Punku is precisely 984 yards to the south of the present village of Tiwanaku and 984 yards to the south-west of the Akapana. With no more evidence than the Indian belief in mountain spirits and an open direction to the sunrise, I can only speculate that the Tiwanakans sited the Puma Punku specifically. Some of the latest 1 : 50,000 maps of Bolivia confirm the azimuths. The Puma Punku has a latitude of 16° 33′ 30″ south. Illimani stands approximately sixty miles to the east, and Pico del Indio, the highest point (20,893 feet), is at latitude 16° 38′ 40″. The slight skew in the azimuth of the platform would make Puma Punku point to the northern shoulder of the mountain. An alignment with the sunrise over the mountain, which would occur four or five days away from the equinox, would cause the mountain god and the sun god to come together.

But how could the ancient Tiwanakans have determined their north, south, east and west for the Kalassasaya without the aid of the compass? I remembered my conversation with Gerald Hawkins on the Pampa de San José. 'Bisecting the angle derived from the rising and setting of a star will find north,' he had said.

Later our discussion had progressed to the equinoctial line with the sun rising due east and setting due west – or even a variation of bisecting the angle from an observer to the two extremes of the sun on one horizon. As I had seen in Cuzco the Incas had recognized the solstice. So I wondered if the builders of Tiwanaku had also managed it four or five centuries earlier. According to one anthropologist, the modern Aymara recognize the solstice in relation to fixed geographical points, and at least one authority, Adolph Bandelier, who visited Lake Titicaca at the end of the last century, said the Indians had five ceremonial directions: the four corners of the place where they lived, and the centre.

Marion meanwhile had returned to the Kalassasaya where she hoped the sun would be striking the face of the famous decorated archway,

The Sun Gate stands in the north-west corner of the Kalassasaya, and a photograph taken early in the present century shows that archaeologists found the ten-ton slab of andesite in two pieces. Much speculation surrounds the apparent orderly arrangement of the carved winged figures flanking the intricately shaped central face. Was it a calendar? One theory considers how the Tiwanaku year was based on the movement of the sun, and suggests that the central dominant figure represents the March equinox, the lower head the September equinox, and the heads at extreme left and right the summer and winter solstices.

known by local tradition as the Gate of the Sun. It was carved from a single block of reddish-grey andesite but no one knows exactly how it stood at the height of the Tiwanakan civilization. A photograph taken early this century shows the arch in two pieces, though more recently the fractured pieces, estimated to weigh ten tons, have been hauled into the original shape. An intricately carved frieze spans the arch. A central godlike figure standing on two short legs is flanked by four rows of tiny winged figures. Did the brooding face represent Con Ticci Viracocha, the creator, or was it an earlier god of the Aymara, Thunupa? Someone long ago had even described the frieze as a calendar and so it has remained in the popular mind, but without a conclusive explanation for its function.

Not very much is known about the Aymara in the pre-Inca period as, by the time the Spanish chroniclers arrived, the Aymara beliefs had been coloured by Inca beliefs, perhaps to the extent of raising Viracocha to the position of supreme god. Some tribes possessed temples to the god who 'lived in the sky'. Other temples were dedicated to the sun, and apparently built by the Inca. In the land of the Lupacas a statue stood on a high hill facing east across Lake Titicaca: a tall man flanked one side and a woman the other.

These were relics of the more formal aspects of the state religion. But, as in the Inca religion, day-to-day practices concerned the spirits of the natural world: the hills, springs, stones and other *wak'as*, where one chronicler, Friar Martín de Morúa, described sacrifices being made. The friar, who completed his writing in 1590, gives an often garbled account of the Incas and their customs, but his references to the Aymara are among the few so far discovered. Luckily some of the Aymara customs, with a layer of acculturation, have survived into relatively recent times, and can be seen in practice today.

The drive east from Tiwanaku fifty miles to La Paz takes about one and a half hours in reasonable weather. We were fortunate: the sun shone, the rivers were low and we had no problems. We had both driven the road innumerable times but we never tired of one particular view: we could not resist stopping at the single high point in the journey from which you can look across to the snow-clad Cordillera Real, the eastern of the two ranges that make up the Andes at this point, and one of the finest mountain chains in South America. We were not disappointed. The view was magnificent, even more dramatic than we had ever seen before: the white snow blanket reached low so that the long crenellated range stood out sharply against the darkening afternoon sky. Mount Illimani stood at the south-eastern end of the La Paz valley and beside it, but a step lower, the huge, gently sloping snowfield of Mururata glistened at 19,250 feet. From there until the far distant north, mountain peaks stood shoulder to shoulder. They had indeed once represented a long line of Aymara gods.

Marion selected a lens from her camera bag. 'There was a freak snow storm a few days ago,' she said.

Snow at that time of the year, June, is unusual. Now the air was already so cold that the white blanket would remain into the spring.

La Paz, the world's highest capital city, rests in a deep canyon at the foot of the Cordillera Real. Its height is generally accepted as 11,733 feet, but in recent years some of the suburbs have spread upwards and then outwards on the edge of the *altiplano*, some 1,600 feet higher. In

Father Cobo's time this was a small settlement called Chuquiabo after the river, now written as Choquiapu, which the city straddles. My first call was to the Military Geographic Institute on the river's east bank, not far from the towering new concrete blocks of shops and offices lining the city's main avenue.

The streets were crowded with businessmen, students and shoppers. On many of the corners *mestizo chola* women in traditional derby hats displayed razor blades, soap, oranges, newspapers and iced drinks on low tables in front of them. The particular trade is apparently determined by the location: along one street you encounter four women in a row dispensing drinks while, two blocks away, it seems that all the razor blades in the world are piled on half a dozen stalls.

Cartographers of the Military Geographic Institute have spent the last twenty years compiling a definitive map of Bolivia. The task is a difficult one. The country is enormous, some 412,162 square miles, approximately twice the size of France, and to date the work is almost two-thirds completed. Several years ago, when Marion and I had been searching for breeding colonies of the world's rarest flamingo in the south of the country, the Institute had helped us with maps and route information. At that time, one senior officer, knowing of my interest in the Nasca lines, referred me to a place he had discovered where many lines or tracks appeared to meet. The spot he had described for me was over a hundred miles from the place where I later saw the hilltop offering, but his pictures revealed many more lines than I could ever have guessed would exist, and even more surprisingly, some of these were relatively close to La Paz itself. Then I had no time to take the research any further, and anyway the maps of the area had not been completed. But while I was in hospital back in London I studied those photographs long and hard.

At the barrier gate entrance to the Army headquarters a soldier checked my appointment details and identification before allowing me through. Once again the surveyors made me feel at home. I was told simply to ask for what I wanted and they would search their files. So I described the area I wanted to look at. I was in luck. It had just been mapped and at a fairly large scale, 1 : 50,000. And that meant that the all-important astronomical 'true north' could be quickly established.

A lieutenant collected the sets of pictures for the area and helped me to lay them out on a table. The pictures had been taken as overlapping pairs which a stereoscope could convert into instant 3D. The final result, a huge mosaic, represented 60,000 square miles of the Andes.

First of all I checked my bearings against a larger map. As clear landmarks I first chose Lake Titicaca, which was easy to find on both the pictures and the map, and the volcano Sajama, at 21,390 feet Bolivia's second highest mountain. It appeared as a large white splodge against the photographic grey but the outline of the snowcap could be clearly seen from directly overhead. Sajama is in the western *cordillera* of the Andes, just inside Bolivia's frontier with Chile, and ninety miles from the sea. A sight line from La Paz to Sajama, roughly 130 miles, forms the base of a large triangle with Lake Titicaca at the northern apex. The main concentrations of 'lines' fell within a hundred miles each side of the base of this imaginary triangle.

It took three full days to weed out the most promising areas from the photographs. In some places the lines simply formed crazy networks, jumbles of directions that would take years of research to unravel. In others the lines were long, very straight and isolated one from another. There were also sets of parallel lines and complexes, as at Nasca, that looked like spokes radiating from hubs. In short, many of the pictures resembled the Pampa de San José. There were no large cleared areas however, nor animal figures in the pictures I checked.

An excellent mirror stereoscope made the relief 'pop up' like the cardboard cut-outs in a child's book, and as my eyes grew accustomed to the scale of the ground features I was able to interpret the numerous terminal points of the lines. Hills and rocky places comprised the majority and what looked like tiny white dots on the hills or at the ends of the lines were small white-painted *capillas* or little chapels which are sacred to the modern Indian inhabitants.

Dr Alfred Metraux, the renowned French anthropologist, had travelled in this area in the late 1920s and his descriptions of lines and small hilltop chapels reflected precisely what I could see in the pictures. He wrote of the cult 'of the mountains' that was 'so alive among the Aymara', and of the way it was revealed in small chapels or oratories perched on summits, 'often with difficult access'. Of special interest to me was his description of the lines as seen from the hills, which bore many similarities to Maria Reiche's early remarks on Nasca. In these deserts he saw 'paths' that 'converged towards the chapels like spokes of a wheel' and 'paths' that led straight to the chapels 'without regard to the roughness or incline of the ground'. But like all the researchers so far he was unable to discern the precise use of the lines.

When I first read Dr Metraux's account – it had been presented to the Society of Americanists in 1932 – my immediate interest lay in his opinion that the lines were 'paths' and in his comments on their straightness. He had, of course, seen them only from the ground, where indeed they do, as at Nasca, appear as paths. The 'line' concept has only arisen since the beginnings of air travel and aerial photography. From my earlier experience in the high Andean deserts I knew how the paths had been made by clearing (and it must have been quite deliberate) the coarse, slow-growing tola bushes (*Lepidophyllum*), the characteristic plant of the area. On the photographs the straightness of the paths was obvious – they crossed all kinds of obstacles with that same unnerving precision of the Nasca lines. Once more the question: why so straight?

Had the lines been built by the Aymara tribes? Tiwanaku proved that geometrical precision was within the capabilities of the early inhabitants of this area of Bolivia, but with such a confused history of conquest, reconquest and the determined Spanish efforts to eradicate paganism, I guessed there was bound to be only a very garbled documentary explanation for the shrines and lines laid out on the photographs in front of me.

Ideally I now needed to find a small village with a few simple paths in use within living memory. If such a place could be located, then the system could be dissected, piece by piece: not physically, that was for archaeologists. There were now numerous indications, however, that some answers could be gleaned from among the Indians themselves and the religion they practised even today.

8 The Ethno-answer

It was mid-June and the air was cold. The sun had just risen above the rim of the eastern *cordillera* when I walked across the tarmac at La Paz airfield. With Peter Williams, a British engineer from Shropshire, a long-time friend and mountaineer, and our young Bolivian pilot, Oswaldo, I planned to fly over the *altiplano* in the region of the Sajama volcano, to check if the rivers and mudflats were passable on the ground and, if possible, to pinpoint from the air some of the lines I had seen on the Bolivian Military Geographic Institute photographs.

Peter had lived in La Paz for ten years and was a veteran of many expeditions, including one that scaled Mururata in the Cordillera Real. That mountain now stood behind us, shining white with virgin snow after the early falls. I envied him that experience. To get the same clarity of view as was possible from the top of Mururata, we were going to fly with the door of our plane off.

Peter was wearing two anoraks and a down-filled purple duvet jacket. Even his broad frame and six feet two inches seemed modest beside our pilot, who had to bend double to climb into the tiny turbine-powered Cessna that had been prepared for the high altitude. We would be flying at nearly 18,000 feet and banking between tall peaks in order to get the best view of the lines. We stowed our gear carefully under the seats, tying safety cords from the cameras to the chair fastenings: Nikons were too precious to lose. After a brief wait for clearance, Oswaldo turned on to the main runway, at 13,330 feet the highest commercial strip in the world. The powerful engine whined as the propeller grabbed at the thin air and we were quickly up and away on course for Sajama.

The sky over the *altiplano* was extraordinarily clear. On my right, Lake Titicaca lay as a silver streak and, over Oswaldo's shoulder, the white cone of Sajama appeared merely as a blob on the horizon 130 miles away. Below, the fenceless fields of the Aymara lay neatly ploughed and planted. Surface stones had been gathered into heaps looking like so many grey pimples rising in orderly rows and I was reminded of Duncan Masson's theory of the origin of the stone heaps on the Nasca desert.

It was an hour's flight to Sajama and I used the time to check the daylight with an exposure meter, noting the range for each type of film – there would be no time for such niceties once we reached the mountain. Colour, black and white and two rolls of infra-red which needed a special filter. Where was it? I cursed my carelessness. Oh no, not still in the jeep! Peter saw my frenzy with benevolent amusement. He put his hand into his bag.

'Is this what you're looking for?' He reached over my shoulder and shouted in my ear, 'I found it under your seat.' With relief I transferred it to my own bag.

As we marvelled at the magnificent *altiplano* scenery, I leaned over Peter's shoulder to look with him at a line of forty or fifty beasts stretched over a hill like a row of brown, black and white dots, with the even smaller figure of the herder close behind them.

'That must be Tiwanaku over there,' I said.

Peter pointed to a village beyond some hills to the north.

'If the lines *are* there and not just scratches on the negative,' Peter joked, 'we'll find them.'

A path leads across the hills and ravines of the central Andes.

I was fully confident, as on my last jet plane journey into La Paz, from Buenos Aires, I had seen some lines clearly, even through the sealed windows.

Our first distance marker was a low range of red sandstone hills twenty-five miles out, the same sedimentary rocks used by the builders of Tiwanaku. Next we crossed a wide river, the Desaguadero or 'outlet river' that flows from Titicaca and drains into a shallow lake some 160 miles south into the *altiplano*. Now, at last, I knew we were getting to our goal.

Below us, on either side of the river, the land was relatively level, but the few hills were deeply dissected by small tributaries which were noticeably dry. Four hundred years ago the Pacaje, an Aymara sub-tribe, lived in this part of the Andes, and the name survives as a present-day province of Bolivia. Similarly, another area, today known as Carangas, south-west of the same river, is named after the Caranga, another Aymara-speaking tribe. In both areas I had seen or been told of lines which, in turn, had been confirmed by the photographs. With our total 'scanning facility' of six eyes, I reckoned it would not be long before we sighted some.

Los Carangas, using the old name for the land, was once much larger than the present province marked on the map. In about 1620, according to chronicler Vásquez de Espinosa, it was 'one of the largest and finest in all Pirú'. Parts of it were very rich and it was particularly famous for its llamas, the 'best and sturdiest to be found'.

As far as I had been able to discover, the ancient pathways had not been mentioned in the historical records of this area, though here for some reason they survived more clearly than in most other places. One reason perhaps is the semi-desert character of the place; both dryness and high altitude reduce plant growth and, as the paths were made by clearing the sparse slow-growing vegetation, I suspected the growth was slow to regenerate. Another possible cause strangely paralleled Nasca. The province was virtually depopulated in the sixteenth century when the Indians were enslaved to work the Spanish silver mines, particularly Potosí, then the largest source of silver in the New World. The enslavement, known as the *Mita*, was widespread and entailed drafting whole villages of men, women and children who, according to one account, trudged to the mines in slow funereal processions to the sound of women crying and sombre music.

Oswaldo turned slightly north from his bearing on Sajama: the volcano, thickly snow-capped, was looming only thirty miles ahead. I

Mount Sajama, a volcano more than 20,000 feet high, was the landmark.

peered out of the open door from my seat in the middle of the 'plane facing the opening. I pulled the anchorages of the nylon harness for reassurance: a simple seat belt would have been totally inadequate for the next manoeuvre.

With the coolness of a professional hunter, Oswaldo positioned the plane. He turned to me shouting above the rush of air.

'A straight track is below now. Hold it, don't photograph yet.'

'Where's the track?' I had to yell to make myself heard.

The young pilot directed my attention somewhere under the right wing. Satisfied with his position, he turned. The right wind dipped and instantly the empty door space lay open, straight to the ground. Instead of sky and the horizon, the earth below was laid out like a map. A straight line pointing like the second hand of a clock was going backwards, eleven, ten, nine, eight o'clock. How long could he hold the turn? We were at 16,000 feet. I snatched several shots, the photography was of secondary importance. Where did the line go? Seven, six o'clock, five – we had done almost the full 180 degrees and Oswaldo was now

Radiating lines, grids of lines and lines crossing on a hillside, many of them drawn over rough ground with uncanny precision. They lead to ancient holy places including hills, springs and narrow gullies. Many of the lines are old and the photograph on the left reveals that sand dunes have moved and obliterated the paths in many places.

pulling out of the turn. No wonder he had been so highly recommended to us.

'*Que macanudo hombre* – great stuff!'

The line rose slowly with the horizon again and led to a ravine between weirdly eroded rock pillars. To get a view of the other end Oswaldo made one broad climbing turn until we could see the full length of the track: it lay across an uneven valley floor, but straight as a tightly drawn string, about three miles long. At the far end, a small house stood in total isolation. Only a dark patch of llama dung or *taquia*, in a round, stone-built corral nearby, showed that the house and the line were still in use.

'Do you want to go around again?' Oswaldo yelled enthusiastically. 'There's another track over there.'

I motioned him to head onwards. I had been told of some lines on the Sajama volcano which was now very close. As we approached the white peak, which dominates that western edge of the Andes, Oswaldo began the climb upwards to Sajama and five smaller peaks alongside it. Enormous beds of the pale pink ignimbrite rock were spread below the volcanoes, spewed out by them like foam from a shaken beer bottle and solidified fifteen million years ago.

A line leads to a flank of a mountain at 15,000 feet in the western *cordillera* of the Andes.
Right – a track almost twenty miles long crosses a hilly landscape at over 13,000 feet. The path leads between two low hills.

Minutes later we flew between the peaks, their black ashy sides streaked with sulphurous yellow. Near the craters, snow clung to the rocks and all but the most precipitous slopes. Peter pointed to a wisp of steam rising like an Indian smoke signal from the summit of Cerro Parinacota, a volcano named after a nearby deep blue lake full of pink flamingos.

'Look, a fumarole – fantastic!' That overused word, varied occasionally with the Spanish '*increíble*', came all too easily to us throughout the flight. The views were breathtaking even for seasoned travellers.

Lines led in every direction. All of those I could see were single paths and often led unerringly over hills and gullies. All were apparently clear, so either the vegetation had been reduced by recent clearing and walking, or it had never grown over since the paths were made. Some of the paths led to small, white-painted *capillas*, shrines standing on hilltops; others led into open scrub-covered wilderness and petered out for no apparent reason.

We flew along the west side of Sajama and, after several gravity-defying gyrations, discovered more lines. One led right to the top of another volcano and other paths crossed on hillsides. Spokes lay scattered as though all the wheels of a cart had collapsed at the same time and, as a *coup de grâce*, Oswaldo located one extraordinary line, measuring more than thirty kilometres on a map, dead straight despite hills and other obstructions along its route. From above, it seemed the line must have been made long ago, as it led directly under extensive sand dunes, while what looked like a modern trail followed the principal direction but skirted the dunes before turning to rejoin the old straight path. I thought of Mejía Xesspe. This particular line was a reminder of his report of certain Nasca lines leading under sand, which he felt was an indication of their antiquity.

The ground below was utterly barren and the few villages we flew over were tiny. But, as I had expected, the main dirt road to the Chilean frontier looked sound. A truck 2,000 feet below might have been rocket-propelled from the trail of dust it threw up a mile long behind it. I turned to Peter. He nodded his agreement that the ground conditions were good enough to make our trip overland.

Back in La Paz I turned to a Bolivian friend, Cancio Mamani, for help. He would be a perfect companion on the expedition. He had lived in La Paz for nine years, firstly at school, then college, but he was from an Aymara family in Pacajes and he knew the area dialect. This was particularly important as local variations in certain words had already caused me some confusion when I had been reading early documents.

By remarkable luck his vacation was due. However, when he heard the route we planned to take he looked glum and pulled his coat collar firmly around his ears.

'Oh yes, I know it well.'

I suspected something worse was to come. Perhaps he knew the area too well? Had the people been unhelpful? No, not that at all. It seemed that on his last expedition his jeep had been stuck in a river for two days and he and his companions had had to improvise a camp in temperatures well below freezing. Not an uncommon experience in the Andes, but potentially very dangerous.

'It's cold, Tony, very cold. You'll have to find me a spare sleeping bag.'

Fortunately I had one, as Marion was not coming on the trip – she had to remain in La Paz to research the BBC film. But there was a bleakness about Cancio's words that still made me shiver. It was a couple of years since I had last camped in the central Andes and home comforts make you soft. Peter came up with a good idea: mattresses of three-quarter-inch-thick foam plastic.

'You can buy them in Calle Manco Capac – a busy street well uptown,' he said.

I have always found that large expeditions have inbuilt disadvantages: the daily routine seems bound up with endless logistical problems, food, routes, walking and climbing. The expedition 'mind' collectively becomes too isolated from the land and people around it. This journey, I stressed, would be different: we would travel light and, with Cancio's help, sleep and eat in villages wherever possible. Any measurements and surveying were to be at the simplest level; anything more complex could be achieved by photographic methods later. My aim was to listen to local opinion, recording the data as I found it. But I resented even the technology of the tape recorder as an intrusion.

Leaving La Paz at noon precisely, we headed south. After a couple of hours on smooth tarmac we turned west and crossed the surprisingly broad River Desaguadero and headed out into the high plain which, as we had anticipated, was dry, brown and dusty. Our day's objective was to reach the old curacy of Curuhuara, mentioned in the chronicles: we could rest there and then, the following morning, examine some lines clearly shown on the air photos.

To our surprise, however, we found a line much sooner than we had

The path leads between two low hills.

expected. Peter was driving when we first spotted it and he chose a slight rise just ahead and eased the jeep over a shallow gully into the dry puna grass beside the road. There he stopped. Dust we had sucked along behind us enveloped the cab, and as it settled I opened the right-hand door. Cancio joined me. With a very old pair of Japanese 8 × 50s (Marion had bought them in Panama years ago) I scanned the length of the lines. The straight path was at least two miles long and led from one small *capilla* or shrine to another. Both *capillas* stood on low hills and the nearest was no more than 600 yards away from us. The general direction of the line lay east–west, though, rather than being astronomical, I suspected it had been aimed to point between two volcanic cones that gleamed on the horizon over seventy miles away.

It was time for some gentle exploring. Setting out as briskly as I could across the hard turf, I reached the line in a matter of ten minutes. As I expected, the line was a simple, straight path cleared in the low undergrowth. The ground on the side of the first hill was stony. Lower down, where the terrain was level, it was sandy. On each side the resinous, slightly aromatic *altiplano* tola bush stood waist high. I examined the path carefully. Either the bushes had not regenerated since being cleared long ago, which I found hard to believe, or they had been cleared in fairly recent times: no young plants stood on the track. Alfred Metraux had said in 1932 that 'the paths were well kept'. I could agree – he was describing a region eighty miles to the south, but the evidence in front of me was very similar.

I had joined the path roughly fifty yards from the first *capilla*. Turning to face the hill, I climbed slowly, eyes peeled along the way. Immediately I found some broken terracotta pottery resting in the rutted stony slope. The pieces, all about the size of a crown bottle top, were well scattered, not like the most obvious sherds at Nasca which usually occurred in neat concentrations. However, in a loose comparison, it was worth noting that there was pottery on both sets of lines. Taking care not to disturb it for the archaeologists, I knelt to get a closer look. Cancio stood beside me, watching with amused interest.

'That's money if you know how to use it,' he said.

I turned to him. Did he mean it was worth selling? Surely no one would give anything for that, even if it were centuries old, which I doubted.

He explained. 'They're *jik'illita* and very important in every Aymara community. They have symbolic value, and they're used in a religious festival as money.'

I looked again at the pieces of a broken earthenware pot. As I guessed, they were recent. Later, on other paths, we found more sherds and some of an earlier period, probably Inca. Apparently Cancio's Aymara community held a fiesta on 2 January, like many other Aymara communities. Several days before the fiesta the religious would go to the *capilla* to fast. In his childhood, parents and children would encircle the shrine three times on their knees, under the watchful eye of the patron of the fiesta. When the fast was over, Cancio said, the ladies fetched food in earthen bowls and dishes. In some ritualistic way, not explained precisely, all the pottery was then broken and the pieces offered to the shrine as *jik'illita* or 'money fragments'.

Pieces of clay pot are still used as money during the fiesta of Alicitas, now held in January. Alicitas by tradition is a fertility or propitiary festival, held for Eq'eq'o, the god of fortune and prosperity. It is one of the most ancient Aymara traditions and, according to various anthropologists, is accompanied by considerable sexual licence among the young Aymara.

Rigoberto Paredes, an eminent Bolivian writer on Aymara mythology, tells us that Alicitas was held at the winter solstice in former times. Farmers would offer any strange fruits from their harvest, and the craftsmen their work, such as ceramics, weavings or tiny sculpted figures in mud, tin or lead. If a man had no such offerings to make, he would acquire them with 'little stones' which he would find in the countryside and which had some peculiarity. 'No one would refuse to exchange objects for these, for fear of angering the gods,' Paredes says.

The sixteenth-century extirpators tried unsuccessfully to stamp out the festival before it was re-established in 1781 by Don Sebastían de Segurola, then Governor of La Paz. He changed the date of the festival in the words of Señor Paredes 'from 20 October to 24 January', on which day it is now held annually in La Paz. Everything on sale is in

Miniature pots and pans are among the many items for sale in the Alicitas fair held annually in Aymara towns. At one time these goods were bought and sold with pot sherds and though this is rare today, some of the old tradition has survived in the mountains where the villagers build miniature houses at special places. The festival is held for the good-luck fertility spirit Eq'eq'o and images of the spirit are kept in most Bolivian houses – they are adorned with miniature goods representing the owners' material wishes.

miniature, even specially printed money in bundles of hundreds of thousands of dollars. The festival survives also in villages, the Indians building small stone houses which they fill with miniature clay animals, small utensils and other objects they hope to acquire in the next year. These items are still bought with the broken pieces of clay produced in the *capillas*.

Since the days when Tiwanaku was at its zenith, the Aymara religion has passed through various stages of acculturation. With each successive change certain new beliefs have been incorporated: the sun, Viracocha, the Incas, then the Spanish sixteenth-century conversions. Yet much of the mythology has lasted well into the twentieth century.

I continued on up the hill to take a close look at the *capilla*. It was a tiny square edifice four to five feet high, made from pieces of flat rock and small mud bricks of three distinct levels. A whitewash, probably of locally fired stone, had been recently painted over the outside. Just as Alfred Metraux reported, an opening or niche faced east. The top was surmounted by a small adobe cross and inside a few blobs of candle grease were the only sign of any recent tokens of respect. On the ground to the west side of the shrine, a group of five stones, each the size of an orange, lay neatly together.

When we reached our destination, Curahuara, an hour after sunset, it was bitterly cold. The streets were quiet: all the doors were firmly closed and even the sound of our jeep rumbling along the narrow dusty tracks provoked no movement that we could see. Our powerful lights picked out the brown adobe mud brick walls of the houses standing close on either side of the vehicle, the only sidewalk being a roughly made path around the edge of the old cobbled square. Cancio directed the way.

'Past the church.' It was white, adobe, and cast a massive shadow in the lights. 'Now turn right.' The street narrowed and it was Peter who spotted the small wooden signboard – 'Pension Curahuara'. He pulled in close to the mud wall and stopped the engine with the kind of finality that comes after six hours at the wheel.

'What's the betting they've run out of tea? If we can stay here, let's unpack the gear before supper.'

One room opened directly to the street and was lit only by a single, hissing oil lamp. The mantle glowed brilliantly, casting a shaft of light into the cold street. An Aymara lady, speaking Spanish, invited us inside. 'Buenos noches, señores – hace frio.' ('It's cold.')

The room was simply furnished with wooden chairs and small plastic-topped tables. Calendars advertising beer, Japanese motorcycles and motor tyres decorated the walls. As we entered, Cancio spoke in Aymara to another woman standing behind a low wooden counter. Could we stay? He was rubbing his hands to revive the circulation.

He nodded across to us and explained, 'From Inglaterra.' Then he chatted on to the lady who was obviously an old friend. She nodded her bowler hat, which meant we had somewhere to sleep. Some people appeared from a yard at the back of the house and offered us a choice of chicken and rice, or a chicken soup with rice. 'Yes, we have beer. With rice or chicken?'

Cancio sorted out the confusion and Señor Perez, the owner, well-built and wearing a heavy scarf tucked under a brown worsted jacket, soon cleared an empty room for us. It was large and our strips of foam and sleeping bags would fit side by side.

Over supper I made a few references to my interest in astronomy, paths and the hills. I got little response but when Cancio took a cue, and explained to his friends in Aymara my obviously strange interest in the paths and their directions, they were a little more forthcoming. Not much was known – 'the older people perhaps', and some said spirits lived there. Their information seemed as confusing as the sources.

Next morning we were up soon after dawn. Three chickens that had somehow missed the supper pot crouched for warmth in a patch of sunlight by the door. We reloaded the jeep. Our first stop was at the foot of a strangely shaped hill rising perhaps 200 feet above the village. It was called Monterani, after its resemblance to a Spanish helmet. A whitewashed *capilla* stood on the summit. With the glasses I searched for a route: several almost sheer cliffs of dark volcanic rock made an approach from the east difficult, so I chose a longer way around, well to the south. 'The shrine is much larger than the one we saw yesterday,' I commented to Peter, who was studying the direct ascent route with a mountaineer's eye. He turned to the air photos and tried to find our exact position.

'I reckon we're here.' He pointed to a small spur ahead of us. He was right. 'If you go less than a hundred yards you'll find it,' he muttered, peering at the picture with a small lens. Then he twisted the photo against a compass and the landscape. 'Over there, there's the line.' We headed towards the spot, keeping note of the hill, now on our right.

It was an ideal location for checking our bearings on the ground. I had a good mental picture of the azimuths for the sun *extrema*, and anything more complicated could be done later. According to the pic-

tures, which had been taken at the beginning of the Bolivian mapping programme, the line we were heading for began at a small *capilla*, perhaps no more than a large whitewashed stone. We quickly located the place: a square shrine somewhat smaller than the one I had visited the day before. But only traces of the whitewash remained and no trace at all of the line.

It was a stiff climb to the top of the hill. Looking down to the tola-covered *pampa* below, I saw vestiges of straight sections of track in mottled brown and green patches where the hardy bushes and puna grass had regrown. The discovery, or more particularly the disappearance, of the path was important. In less than twenty-four hours I had seen two sites: at one, the path had been kept clear; at the other, where the locals expressed ignorance of the traditions, it had almost vanished. Did this account for the mysteriously invisible lines of Cuzco, the forty-two *ceques* of Father Cobo? I had asked about *ceques* in La Paz and heard varying opinions. Dr Metraux had written about them as pertaining to one village well to the south-west of here. All that, however, was to come later. We had many more paths to visit, and leaving the hill we headed into the rocky desert towards Sajama.

Overhead the sky was a clear, dark blue, and near the sun it darkened to a deep purple. The intense rays were already burning my face and

An aerial photograph taken in 1963 shows paths to the hill: these are now overgrown with grass and tola bushes.

hands and for me the only safeguard was a special high-altitude filter cream. Both Peter and Cancio were well accustomed to the strong ultra-violet and needed no such protection.

The dirt road narrowed to little more than the width of the jeep and followed the winding course of a small river for twenty miles, before ascending gradually in a steep-sided valley. All the way the ravine had been carved from the pink ignimbrite of the volcanoes, but Sajama was still out of sight. This was the road we had seen from the air and eventually it reached a gently inclined plateau with the giant snow-covered profile of Sajama towering at the upper, distant end.

For two hours the going was hard; the dusty surface gave way to hard rock which the road builders had been unable to level. The ignim-brite's fractured surface had eroded into an irregular mass of holes and ruts which tested Peter's patience and concentration for two hours. His face was grim. If it had not been for the mountain beckoning ahead of us, he would have turned back.

'Shall I take over?' I asked. After all, with Marion I had driven from end to end of the Andes.

'No – you watch for lines,' he answered quietly.

We made Sajama village at the foot of the mountain by nightfall.

'Tea?' said Peter hopefully. 'Weak and no sugar, please.'

A path from the village to a hilltop shrine.

'No,' I forecast, 'it's beer and chicken soup.'

We were offered lodging by the local police post. And my forecast was all too correct.

Sajama village is isolated, half hidden in a valley between volcanoes, and it marked the furthest point of our journey; the Chilean frontier is about seven miles away. From the air I had seen some long lines near the village, especially two that led to hilltops. One of these ran straight for more than a mile and crossed another hill on the way.

'Cold?' I inquired with mock nonchalance as we sat down to eat.

'No,' said Peter, 'just don't break your spoon on the soup when it freezes.'

I was tempted, but decided against spoiling his supper with a story of cannibalism I had culled from the manuscript journal of Adolph Bandelier. According to his account of an incident somewhere near Sajama in 1898, three prisoners of the Aymara were ripped up alive and their entrails thrown on a fire. Later their bodies were roasted and eaten.

We had reached 14,000 feet and the temperature was at a miserably cold minimum of minus ten degrees C. But as we had seen from the air, lines led everywhere and most frequently to hills and far up mountain sides. Some of them lay in Chile and would have to wait for later investigation.

We explored a total of twenty-two different sites in the area and, as I suspected, hills and stones were the most numerous terminal points. The hills were usually crowned by white *capillas* often topped with a cross, signifying their Spanish connection; they could have been built at any time within the last 400 years, since the Christian church was established. Or, of course, they could have been laid out in antiquity, and later supplied with marks of the new religion.

Today the hills with shrines are usually called *calvarios*, as in the Christian Indian mind they now symbolize Calvary. Sometimes a row of small white-painted shrines set in hillsides represent 'stations of the Cross' and prayers are made at each one during the slow ascent to the highest. For the ancient Aymara, according to Cancio, the hilltops, known as *silus*, were once sacred places, where spirits of some undefined character lived. Early anthropological research compared the Aymara belief in spirits of high places with the Quechua belief in *apus*: the higher the hill the more powerful was the spirit. If applied to Nasca, this belief explained those lines that led over one hill to another, higher one. According to the custom in the old region of Carangas, the highest hill within an undetermined radius of the Indian was the most respected *silu* and, if the path led over lower hills to reach the most distant observable *silu*, then intermediate shrines were automatically established on the way. *T'aki* was the generic name for all manner of tracks; *silu t'aki* was a path to a *calvario* (sometimes *calvari t'aki*), and various other words preceded *t'aki*, denoting the kind of place to which the track led.

From the volcano-rimmed heights of the western *cordillera* of the Andes, we descended to the open *altiplano* once more. The rough road crossed dunes, vast open *pampas* covered by low tola and marshes dried hard by desiccating frosts. We crossed several shallow sluggish rivers, no more than thirty inches deep, their banks lined with ice, even though we were near the equator, in the tropics. It was intolerably austere.

We were rewarded, however, with the sight of many lines. Often the *t'akis* or paths led from the simple adobe-built churches out to hilltops in the *pampa* beyond. The lines, like those at Nasca, crossed space well

away from inhabited areas and, as well as hills, there were piles of stones. Sometimes I found these on the hilltops. Simple cairns, probably old, lay half-concealed beside small whitewashed shrines; in one place, a modern shrine, a pile of stones and a group of crudely shaped stones were arranged beside one another on a hilltop. On the *pampa*, and in places where one would not expect stones, we located rounded stones carefully piled about eighteen inches high.

'What are those piles?' I asked Cancio.

'Old holy places,' he replied.

The cult of the stone is widespread among Andean Indians, and mention had often been made in reports and chronicles of the continued importance of stones in Aymara religion and lore. It stems from

their belief that the stone is an essential material of creation. As Rigoberto Paredes says, 'They believe that God made man, not in mud, but in stone, and that they are descended from these men of stone.' He elaborates by pointing out that the most important *wak'as*, idols and *conopas* (household gods) were all of stone.

Initially the *altiplano* stone piles and those at Nasca seemed very similar, but with Cancio's help my untrained eye gradually began to identify three different types of *altiplano* stone piles. All were *wak'as*. Perhaps the various stone piles at Nasca could also be classified into different types.

We discovered that someone was still respecting this *q'ontu* or holy place on a low promontory.

In one remote place on the distant *altiplano*, I was shown a stone heap on a hill by a friendly villager. He said it was a *q'ontu* – a special sacred spot – and coca was left there by 'the old people'. Resting between the stones were no more than a dozen leaves but they were fresh, or at least still pale green, and were stuck together on a lump of grease. Llama fat, I was told. The Aymara name is *lamp'u*, or *hunto*, and it has been a common offering to spirits since Inca days. According to Rigoberto Paredes, a llama is sacrificed, cleaned and then the breast is given to the white magician or *Paquo*. I reflected that coca had been found at Collique, and I had been told to look to 'the Indian mind'.

A second type of stone pile was a place where a spirit resided and a third, called a *tiyaña*, was at a place to stop or rest on the way to the *silu* or *calvario*. Alternatively, as one villager volunteered, it was a place 'to sit and think'.

Other *wak'as* include places struck by lightning, or hit by meteorites, places where a child was born feet first or with a hare-lip and even places where certain llamas were born or conceived. In fact, anything unusual was deemed sacred. Many of the Aymara *wak'as* would never have existed on the Nasca *pampas*, springs and trees among them, but stones and stone heaps were there in abundance. These stones and stone heaps are one of the features on the Nasca desert that all the experts have noticed and felt compelled to explain in different ways.

As we moved deeper into the flat expanse of the *altiplano*, I sensed that the entire problem of lines and sacred places must rest squarely on the shoulders of the ancient Indian. I could pose the question 'Why are these stones, boulders, llama corrals, houses, tombs and other *wak'as* so placed?' But there seemed to be no more precise answer than 'They say a spirit lives there.' Or frequently, 'A spirit used to be there.'

The spirits of places were most important in the hierarchy of the Aymara religion and were ranked according to their power. Among the most sacred were the spirits of high places, followed by the spirits of lakes and rivers, and finally house spirits or *uiwiri*. The most important spirits, *acacila*, were generally not malevolent and were personified as invisible old people, usually men. The *acacila* of the mountains controlled rain, hail and frost. Winds came from the great volcanoes. The positioning of these sacred places was not precise. They were as confusing as the ends of a rainbow, or the places where lightning had struck twice. I concluded that the Aymara world is so thickly populated with supernatural beings that it is virtually impossible to separate them one from another. Gerald Hawkins and María Rostworowski had, from

In a remote part of the old land of the Caranga we are shown a *tiyaña* (resting place) at the end of a straight path cut through tola bushes.

the different standpoints of astronomer and ethnohistorian, advised exploring 'the Indian mind'. But was that mind too profound and remote to understand? Was it possible for a twentieth-century scientist to analyse the spirits of an ancient culture?

Our next stop was at a village described in the chronicles as Turque. Nearby, the air photographs had shown one extraordinary line, well isolated and beginning close to a church as a single path (or possibly two, almost parallel, paths). The line led west–east for nearly five miles across a flat tola-covered *pampa* to a range of low sandstone hills. Seen from the church, the sun would rise above the end of the line at specific times of the year and, of course, the moon would rise in the same general direction on other dates, as would the planets and some stars.

One morning, waking from a comfortable night in the local store-keeper's store-house after now-regular supper of chicken and spicy red sauce or *aji* (chili pepper), we started off towards the sandstone hills shortly before sunrise. Peter, well-bearded, steered carefully, hugging the line of an old track. When it led us through an ice-covered river, the ice crunched at the edge, gave instantly and the tyres bit firmly into the bottom only inches below.

'Easy,' he grinned, glad to be moving. 'Now where?' He pointed to two tracks.

'Left,' I said, relying on my compass bearing. The track, a little wider than the jeep, led us through dark green tola bushes, window-high on either side. Other vehicles had used the trail since the end of the rainy season: we could see their rutted tracks in the dry mud surface. Perhaps it was the same truck setting out and returning the same way.

Peter checked our odometer.

'We've done four and a half miles since the river,' he announced.

'Not very much longer to go.' I had been judging the distance from air photographs spread on the dusty front seat beside me. 'In about a hundred yards, the track should veer to the south.' It did, for about five degrees, and then headed towards a low outcrop of the sandstone.

Peter stopped the jeep as soon as we could see the rock. We were at the brow of a gentle sandy slope leading down to a wide, shallow gully. The tola cover continued across its sandy floor to the base of the rounded hump of red sandstone, part of the same formation I had seen at Tiwanaku 100 miles to the north. A narrow path, an extension of the track we had followed, continued straight over the gully, across two low outcrops of rock to a tiny white *capilla* hidden under the lip of the far hill.

The pictures beside me showed at least twenty lines, mostly connecting the hilltops, or from small adobe houses to the hilltops. I had previously decided to check the extent to which each path appeared to have been used, to take some approximate azimuths and to mark the ends of the lines precisely on a large-scale map. The Military Geographic Institute in La Paz had kindly lent a German compass, the size of a small saucer, which could be read to half a degree; and we had brought, from Britain, an electronic measuring device or tellurometer, to measure the exact distances between the shrines and hence calculate angles. At the end of the work, I would have one group of paths carefully plotted, *capilla* to *capilla*, house to hill and so on. The construction date would be missing, so only sun and moon *extrema* would have any meaning.

'U.F.O.s were here for sure,' someone suggested as we moved, laden with gear, to the hill. There were dozens of lines in the area.

'No,' I puffed (talking and walking at over 12,000 feet is hard work), 'that's not the answer and anyway the most mysterious part is the straightness.'

'Shortest distance between two points,' said the engineer flatly.

'All right then, so why are you walking round this rock instead of over the top?' I countered. 'The old path goes straight over it.'

The rocky outcrop I chose as our first measurement point was between twenty and thirty feet high, steep and covered with loose rocks. I scrambled to the top. The line was clearly visible in both directions: a total length of five and a half miles from the church in the village to the white-painted shrine under the lip of the hill. There were other, very clear, lines and some overgrown by the tough resinous bushes. What had made the people of Turque cut these long straight paths to the shrines? Was it the orderly mind of the surveyor? Modern road builders drive tunnels through mountains for practical purposes: traffic does not flow smoothly either up or down a one in four gradient.

We had questioned villagers along the way and Cancio learnt from this questioning that the paths were straight 'when they concerned holy places'. The notion could have been introduced by the energetic Spanish priests who surely would have preached of the biblical 'straight and narrow'. Perhaps they even quoted to the Indians: 'Make straight in the desert a highway for our God' (Isaiah 40.3). But the Nasca lines were laid down before the arrival of the priests.

Long straight paths, one more than 5½ miles long, lead across a plain over 12,000 feet high, to low hills and then onwards to a prominent crag. The general direction is east from a church in a village and we made measurements to plot the lines and their terminal points. Air photographs and accurate compass bearings taken on the ground gave the azimuths of the paths looking from the village (or individual houses) to the distant shrines.

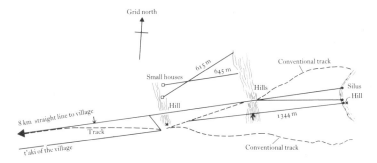

The paths photographed from an altitude of 5,000 feet.

The paths lead to a group of hills.

Shrines on the horizon were visited by the Aymara on specific days.

We checked the length of the paths, shrine to shrine.

Straightness for whatever reason was important to the Indians, and making straight paths would not have been difficult. Even the very long line we had seen on our flight had purpose: it was a special route along which the Indian llama herders travelled. I was told the journey could take four or five days, and as one Aymara said – they were special *uywa t'aki*.

When we asked the purpose of the *capillas* and other *wak'as* or shrines, an Aymara confirmed: 'Yes, these are stopping places on the way.' It seemed clear enough. But why did the lines pass *over* all those hills, straight to the horizon? He could not know that from 10,000 feet overhead the lines were so straight a ruler could be laid against them and no deviation would show. When I checked the line there was an answer. The top of a hill shimmered on the horizon as a mirage from a long way into the desert. The curvature of the earth is such that to see a point on the ground of the same altitude thirty-seven miles away, you have to be 1,000 feet above the surface at the point of observation. Put another way, the top of a hill 1,500 feet high at the end of a twenty-mile line would be visible in the clear *altiplano* air. If cairns had been established on the lower intervening hilltops when the route was laid down, it would not have been difficult to attain such straightness. This technique was certainly not beyond the ability of the early Andean people. The straightness between the starting point and the distant mountain might have been achieved as one man, walking well ahead of a long line of llamas, established cairn after cairn on the way to the highest sight point, many miles ahead. Even the fact that the llama, a sacred animal, will walk directly over a hill may have contributed to the Indians' reasoning.

We had been concentrating on our maps and photographs. Peter had set up the tellurometer.

'We'll check that line, then trace its path.'

I heard Cancio speak in Aymara and I turned to see that we had been joined by a man on a bicycle. Cancio asked his name.

'Rosales,' he replied and we shook hands all round.

Señor Rosales, wearing a machine-made pullover and large cowboy-style hat that was entirely out of place in the remote Andes, was rightly curious. Were we geologists? Some had looked for oil here only a year ago. His home was over the brow of the hill, he told us. He spoke Spanish and like many people in the highlands had been to school and travelled to the 'big' town 100 miles away. He had bought his bicycle there.

I showed him the air photograph. Apparently he understood it, because, pointing to a dot, he laughed and said, 'My house. How small!' Then he held the photograph gently and peered with interest at its contents.

'An aeroplane flew over here yesterday,' he said. He obviously thought it had been us. 'At about one in the afternoon,' he added. We continued chatting, explaining our interest in the *t'akis* and the *silus*. Cancio asked if he could help. No rocks, no drilling, we just wanted information, some dates.

I reasoned that the seventeenth-century priests had countered the old religion with many Spanish beliefs. Syncretism is the word used by anthropologists, and in Andean terms it meant that they had superimposed Christian festivals on the festival dates of the old Andean calendar, almost solstice for solstice. Señor Rosales told me the dates when prayers were said at the various shrines: these were saints' days in the modern calendar. It was a long shot, but one I felt was worth trying: 'Did the sun rise over the horizon near the shrine on the day the shrine

Rows of ancient burial towers, or *chullpas*, are among the few remains of the ancient tribes of the *altiplano*.

was now venerated?' If a sun azimuth matched a shrine exactly it would be no more than chance, as the calendars are so confused. But a line to a hill still venerated on solstice and equinox dates would be a sign that the people who made the line had built it along astronomical principles.

'That temple and that line belong to the village.' Señor Rosales pointed high up on the distant hill. 'That's used on Corpus Christi' (the Thursday following Trinity Sunday).

'The village?' I asked, and he pointed to the way we had come.

'Do the people come here at Corpus?' 'They used to – but not any more. They've stopped it' (the practice). 'There used to be ten or twelve people coming, then there was a fiesta on both ends' (– at the shrine and in the village).

The other shrines – their dates?

He explained that his *t'aki* led to a shrine for San Felipe, 'a little saint' – 1 May. He pointed to a shrine and a *t'aki*.

'How about those hills there and there?' I pointed to the north and south. 'Those are 25 July, Santiago' (St James).

'Is there a *t'aki* to that one?' Peter asked.

'Yes, there's a *t'aki*,' Señor Rosales replied.

For the sun it would not work. Two shrines were venerated on 25 July and separated by at least forty degrees of horizon seen from the village. The sun could not rise over the two hills at the same time. And the 1 January and Corpus Christi shrines were only a few yards apart on the same horizon. Nor did the lines point to the three points of solstice and equinox or the two intermediate dates. But the lines did belong to individual families and two belonged to the village.

So what were the names of the hills? Ahead the craggy one with the shrines was called Kuntur Sayt'awi meaning 'resting place of the condor'.

'All the hill?' I asked.

'Yes, all the hill, not just the *silu*.'

Another hill was Quebradilla – 'a little narrow rugged way'; and other names related to colour and shapes. None was named after the sun, moon or stars: the names all concerned the natural earth-bound world around these people of the *altiplano*.

Obviously the customs of the local people were changing. Various new influences were at work and the old traditions were quickly disappearing. In times past sacrifices had been made at a stone on the way to the shrine – the spot he called a '*mis'quala*'.

I asked Señor Rosales if he could remember when it was last used.

'A black and white bull,' he mumbled.

'Was it offered at the side of the stone?' I asked.

'The bones are burnt afterwards,' he continued. This explained the puzzling disappearance of sacrificial remains.

We asked circumspectly if the practices were of importance these days. He shrugged, and replied, quite openly, 'It doesn't matter any more. To my mother it meant a lot, but to me, not.'

9 Return to Nasca

We stopped for the night in a small *altiplano* village close to the foot of a dark hill. Not a chink of light showed from the adobe houses and the small wooden doors of the only shop were firmly bolted. No one would stir now until dawn. While Peter added more antifreeze to the heavy mixture already gurgling in the radiator, Cancio joined me in the empty square beneath the Andean sky, black like matt velvet but speckled with myriads of stars.

I turned to Cancio, his face muffled inside an alpaca wool scarf, and asked: 'What do the Aymara call the sky or space and the stars?'

'Alaq'Pacha – the sky; an undefined place above the earth.' Cancio used an aspirated sound I found hard to copy. 'And the place where you live – the earth – is Aka'Pacha. Stars in general are *wara wara* and the "bright morning" and "evening star" ' (Venus) 'is Ururi.'

The ancient Aymara had worshipped the moon. No wonder: it was almost full, and crisply defined against the night sky. 'That's "pfajjsi" ' (paxsi), Cancio said, pointing to the moon, 'which also means month.' There was another Aymara word for the moon as a god.

Cancio confirmed that Aymara star-lore was extensive, but he could not add much to the skimpy information contained in reference books; even those produced in Bolivia many years ago hold only scraps of information. According to these sources the Coalsack or Manchada Negra was the 'nest of the condor' (the huge Andean vulture with a nine-foot wing span when fully grown, and venerated by both the Quechua and Aymara Indians). The Milky Way was a 'river of stars', or 'the river of Santiago' (St James), the patron saint of Spain, re-emphasizing the extent to which seventeenth-century Christian priests had succeeded in converting the Andean people. On the other hand, the Milky Way was also referred to by a word meaning 'the road to infinity', possibly an indication of an ancient awareness of the immensity of space, or possibly a concept introduced in modern times. Aymara beliefs concerning certain constellations were frequently similar to those attributed to the

Quechua in the early chronicles. One report from this century listed the Magellanic Clouds (two small ghostly patches of light – two small galaxies, companions to our own Milky Way system). But again, I suspected the concept had been introduced by recent investigators.

The Indian words for 'east' and 'west' were derived from the two positions of the sun (*Inti*) and, as historical records explain, the Aymara recognized east as the most important ceremonial direction. One eminent Bolivian writer, however, Rigoberto Paredes, noted in 1920 that the moon was, and possibly still is, the most noticed heavenly body. All aspects of agriculture were supposedly governed by its phases and appearance, but the precise system was unknown.

At one point in our journey across the *altiplano*, I was reminded of the 'flowering cactus calendar' mentioned by the Anonymous Chronicler in the 'Discurso'. We had reached a steep hillside covered by tiny walled field enclosures, known as *aynoquas*, belonging to individual families in a centuries-old system of crop rotation controlled by the old men in the village, the *yatiris* or 'wise ones'. Each walled field contained a single tall cactus plant, growing in one corner. When I asked the reason I was told it was for some unexplained magical purpose.

The chronicler Cieza de León, obviously confused by the local calendars, reported in 1553 that the Collas had a year of 'ten months to ten months'. His statement, together with the Aymara use of '*paxsi*' for

Ancient field enclosures are still used and belong to a centuries-old tradition of crop rotation.

both 'month' and 'moon', has led to a suggestion that if an Aymara calendar existed in pre-colonial times, it might have been a lunar one. I had been on the lookout for lines that would point to the moon, yet of all the lines I had seen in Bolivia, most pointed in the wrong directions. As Gerald Hawkins had commented of the Nasca lines, too many of the lines pointed north and south, well outside the areas of the horizon where most celestial activity occurs.

It is difficult to deduce the ancient Aymara knowledge of astronomy through the several layers of acculturation from the Incas, the Spanish and now the developed world. Indeed I noted that Señor Rosales had told us he used a printed calendar for counting the days. How would his great-grandmother and her ancestors have known on which days to visit the family shrine? The documentary evidence shows that the Incas recognized the solstices, and the Aymara knew the solstice by observing the sun as it moved between certain geographical points. It would have been possible for them to construct lines pointing towards the sun position on the horizon on those dates as solstice markers; but of all the paths I had seen in Bolivia, not one was directed to the solstice or equinox points on the horizon. One grid of three lines led to a hill three degrees south of the December solstice point, and the other terminal points of the same grid were aimed towards a village.

In the tiny square that night, beneath a black and endless sky, I questioned whether the Aymara had in fact once looked skywards for their gods. Who would build lines on the freezing *altiplano* at night in winter? On the other hand, in the warmer months of the year the sky fills with rain clouds. It would, no doubt, have been possible to use bonfires for sighting the shrines – they are a traditional part of the midwinter festival of San Juan. But it did not make sense: as Gerald Hawkins had said, 'Build a fire on the line and you lose sight of the stars.' Perhaps a marker bonfire a long distance away would work. But some of the lines were very long – twenty miles was the longest so far. Perhaps the stars were used as guides for navigation across the featureless plain.

The possibilities were limitless and all largely speculative. I had found no positive evidence to indicate that the lines had either astronomical or calendric significance. Everything I had learnt pointed to a simple, vague religious use of the lines and shrines. I became more convinced that the explanation lay there; that it was essentially very simple. All the shrines or natural objects at the ends of the paths were linked either with modern religion or ancient earth spirits, and the long-established veneration of the latter was well documented.

It had also become clear that *ceques* were connected with shrines on the *altiplano* at least, as indeed Polo de Ondegardo had reported in 1585. In describing a number of different types of *wak'as*, he said, 'All these things were divided by their *ceques* and lines [sc. limits] around each village.' An old Aymara dictionary gave one definition as 'a boundary or limit'.

From Lima to La Paz I had queried the precise meaning of the word *ceque*, and heard several opinions. An initial complication arose because the word has been transliterated in a number of ways and it was difficult to determine with certainty whether the word was derived from Aymara or Quechua. The earliest report of the Cuzco *ceques* was a famous 'Diagram of the Zeques' made by Polo de Ondegardo sometime before 1561. The document has been lost, though Father Cobo's list of the *wak'as*, said to contain the same information, uses '*ceque*'. The 1608 Quechua dictionary of Gonçalez Holguin gives '*ceqque*'; Mejía Xesspe said '*seqe*' and Americanist John Rowe uses '*siq'i*'.

In one mountain region of central Peru, *ziquis* were said to be furrows in a field. The word was not written, and on the *altiplano* I found that the Aymara still use the word *siq'i*. As Cancio explained, 'It's a row or line of things.' Mejía Xesspe had implied straight rows.

'What kind of things?' I asked. 'Were they sacred and in straight rows?' 'The rows are usually straight,' Cancio confirmed, 'when it is a line of sacred places, like stone piles, *chullpas* – the old burial towers – or tiny chapels. But,' he emphasized, 'you can have a *siq'i* of llamas when they are walking across the *pampa* or a *siq'i* of boundary markers – *chutatas*.' (They are also considered as *wak'as*.)

An Aymara linguist and specialist in phonetics in La Paz added to the confusion concerning the more esoteric use of the word *siq'i* by introducing the concept of the space around the objects and the way this was viewed by different Aymara observers. Apparently these variations were recognized by people from certain areas of the *altiplano*.

Essentially, however, *siq'i* was a line or row of anything and I decided to reconsider the simpler concept of *siq'i* we had seen on our *altiplano* journey. Clearly a path was not a *siq'i*; more precisely it was the row of objects it linked. Such a definition worked well in terms of the Cuzco *ceques* I had attempted to trace. The row did not have to be either straight, or long, or sacred; on the other hand it could be all three. Whether the word was used originally in a religious context or simply as a general description of 'line' may never be known. But what did the sixteenth- and seventeenth-century chroniclers see around villages? Probably well-ordered rows of shrines which the Indians said were *ceques*.

The parallel to be drawn between rows of shrines around one particular Andean village and the *ceques* of Cuzco has already been drawn by Dr Metraux who in 1932 said that the string of *capillas* and oratories arranged 'up to six kilometres apart' (3·75 miles) corresponded 'en tout point' with the *ceques* of Cuzco.

I knew the village he described, as I had been there three times, twice with Marion to film flamingos a few miles to the south. It is situated in one of the coldest, most inhospitable areas of the *altiplano*, among volcanoes, salt deserts and icy rivers, and whipped by strong winds. On my visits there I paid no particular attention to the lines of shrines, but I have since learnt from anthropologists that they were established in a particular order and related to the very old kinship groups that survive in the village even in the present day. The ancient community division into two parts, similar to ancient Cuzco and Tiwanaku, has lasted intact there and in many other regions of the mountains, and is now being studied in depth. The east and west sides represent the main division, and though the line between them does not lie precisely north–south, all the houses are arranged in rows facing the rising sun.

Ceques, I concluded, as rows of shrines on the *altiplano*, had been arranged in random directions apparently dependent upon their purpose. As Polo de Ondegardo explained even earlier than Father Cobo, shrines or *wak'as* could be 'springs or fountains of water, or some flat places made on the side of hills or certain special trees, or the places where they sowed maize for sacrifices'.

What then was the possibility that a village or its temple or principal *wak'a* had been carefully sited centuries ago, so that the paths between the shrines led not only to the hills, springs or other natural *wak'as* but were, at the same time, aligned for a calendric purpose with certain venerated objects in the sky? As Gerald Hawkins had shown at Stonehenge, that ancient stone circle would only work astronomically at its specific latitude, 51 degrees north. Similarly, each Andean village would need an arrangement of *wak'as* specific to its site, if it were to work as a system for predicting important celestial activity.

At Tiwanaku, the Temple of the Puma Punku might well have been oriented to the cardinal points and sited to relate to the mountain Illimani, the old village of Tiwanaku (which an early chronicler noted precisely as pointing north) and the Akapana. That kind of positioning would possibly have been of great significance to the early Andean people, but to juggle an entire 360-degree horizon of assorted peaks, the sun, the 18.6 year-cycle of the moon and also the stars seems highly improbable. And what of precession? The moon cycle alone would have been a mind-bender; the priests would surely have suffered 26,000 years of apoplexy awaiting a godly constellation to reappear above some sacred fixed geographical point. No, the alignment of the *ceques* must surely have been as random as all the spirits known to the ancient Indian mind.

The last stage of my journey was to return to Nasca. On the way I planned to visit some remote mountain villages where in the past I had noticed various surviving traces of the ancient religion. From a point where I left my car with a friendly Aymara family beside the road, it was a long walk into the mountains, across a barren sandy upland where once I had spent days filming the small Andean rhea (like a tiny ostrich). I passed through a number of settlements before arriving at the bottom of a wide valley dotted with tola bushes and filled with the whitened puna grass of late winter. A small group of houses stood around the central church. It was exactly as I remembered it but this time my eye caught signs I had not recognized before. Four white *capillas* lay outside the roughly square boundary of the village, and beyond, on the hills and in the valley, stood other small white-painted shrines.

It would have been eerie and totally unnerving had I not experienced it many times before. Nothing stirred as I walked towards the houses. All the doors were closed. The people had seemingly vanished, as from a ghost town: no barking dogs, no scratching chickens, nothing. As I entered the small square, the only sound came from my padding steps on the soft dusty road surface. I listened intently. After a while a door banged: I judged the sound came from somewhere behind a house on the square's north-west corner. Someone was sizing up the visitor.

Curisoity soon overcame the natural Aymara reticence and an old man wearing homeweave trousers entered the square, while a woman, presumably his wife, watched from behind a wall. He spoke in Spanish heavily accented with Aymara. I explained I had to leave before dark and asked him where I could find a *tienda* or small shop selling beer.

Having made my purchase I walked casually around the square. A massive adobe-built church, brilliant white against a deep blue sky, bore no relation to the size of the present village; indeed, when it was

In front of the church a row of sacred places were established long ago with libations, offerings and sacrifices to be made at each in turn.

built under the direction of the Spanish clergy it must have held sway over a large area of the mountains. Also, size almost certainly meant power and was used to impress the Indians. At a distance of about thirty yards from the church door I noticed a low pile of ashes no more than a yard across where an offering had been made to a spirit. In the Indian mind it was a communion with the sacred being, or perhaps a gift, or even a transference of part of the mind to the unknown.

The pyre was still warm, and a wisp of acrid smoke drifted towards me confirming it had been made that day, I suspected at dawn. Without bending to look, I could make out the clear form of bones whitened by the fire: some ribs and one long leg bone, obviously of a llama. I had seen the same scene before, not here, but in several other villages. Normally the flesh would be eaten before the bones were burnt, just as Señor Rosales had said. But it was not the offering or the smouldering ashes which intrigued me. Such offerings have been reported before. But in crude alignment with the ash pile and the church, someone had placed several rough stones in a small conical pile.

The pile was only six inches high, comprising no more than a dozen stones of varying sizes, but the care with which they were arranged had

to imply some special purpose. The stone pile was not the only feature in the simple line. Walking slowly around the square and past the church I realized, first, that the village was very old and, second, that it had been built and organized in a deliberate way. Conscious that I was being watched, I quickly took some photographs which were later interpreted for me.

I learnt that six sacred places led to the church, the seventh in the line, starting from a *silu* on a hill some miles distant. Next was a holy place at one corner of the village (there were four of these places, each used on specific occasions); then the pile of stones; next an adobe-built shrine in front of the church; next the place of the sacrifice, and finally a bloodstained brick-made square, roughly two feet by two, the *mis'quala* or place for an offering. The Indians made offerings and prayers at each place as they respectfully made their way to the church. It was, on a smaller scale, similar to Father Cobo's seventeenth-century description of the holy stopping-places on the *ceques* of Cuzco. Although the order of the shrines was probably coloured by some ideas introduced in the sixteenth century, the ritual was most likely a curious mixture of old and new beliefs that still exists in many parts of the Andes.

I realized suddenly that I was interrupting a special fiesta, and with a quiet 'buenos tardes' to the old man, now joined by a couple of wide-eyed young children, I turned and followed the winding track back into the mountains.

What I had just seen had been described 400 years ago by a priest, Cristóbal de Albornoz, one of the earliest of those dedicated to the extirpation of idolatry. Albornoz, according to Americanist Pierre Duviols, travelled extensively in the south of Pirú and reported both on the extent and the nature of the *wak'as* of the region in a document probably prepared for the contemporary Viceroy, Martín Enriquez. Albornoz said of a *wak'a* in Cuzco called Churuncani Guanacauri (Huanacauri) that 'it was a large stone and all around were many little *wak'as* of stones called *cachauis*'. He also explains that 'all the *wak'as* in the hills or desert, they have around them signs or tokens they call *cachauis* that are signs or tokens of the offerings that are made to these *wak'as*'.

Elsewhere in the same document, entitled 'Direction [*Instrucción*] for the Discovery of all the *Wak'as* in Pirú', Father de Albornoz actually related these small stones – though frustratingly without further description – to the *ceques*. When instructing his clergy he wrote: 'Offerings will be found in such *ceques* or *cachauis*, and it is necessary to destroy them at the same time as the *wak'as* and all with great care.'

Although Cristóbal de Albornoz was writing some fifty years after the conquest of the Incas, it seems likely his interpretation of *wak'as* can be applied to the early Aymara zenith on the *altiplano* at least 600 years before, and the Nasca lines which are even earlier. The veneration of stones by Aymaras and Incas has been well documented and stones and coloured rock have been found in some coastal Nasca graves. Albornoz said the Nasca Indians' *wak'a* was a hill and a stone. He did not mention other *wak'as* but most historians agree that the Indians never revealed all their *wak'as* and, indeed, it would be most unusual for a village to have only one or two.

All the rows of stones, paths and various forms of conceptual paths I had encountered were concerned primarily with *wak'as*. The piles of stones, the place of sacrifice and four other points which formed the 'row of objects' outside the Andean church not only fitted Father Cobo's description of a *ceque*, but conformed with the definition I had been given of a *siq'i*.

On the *altiplano*, *siq'i* could describe a series of cairns at distances of up to about four miles apart and others on hills close together. Sometimes the path between the cairns, or shrines, was straight, sometimes it was not; sometimes it was long, at other times very short. Of which came first, the path or the *wak'a*, the answer would be derived from the use of each *wak'a*. Finally, I wanted to try to relate this information to the Nasca problem. I had a strong impression that the Nasca paths were of lengths varying according to the space they had to fill: air photographs clearly demonstrate this. The long paths often lead from one end of the *pampa* to the other over a distance of several miles, while the shorter paths, somtimes only a few yards long, can lead from a cleared area at the base of a hill simply as far as its summit, or from one cleared area to another.

My conclusions, conjectured as they must be, are not dissimilar from those of some earlier investigators, but I have additional detail. The various stone piles on the Nasca *pampa* are, I believe, ancient *wak'as*, though the Nascas probably used a different word (no one is sure of their language prior to the Inca invasion of the area). These *wak'as* were arranged in lines or rows for which the word *siq'i* is probably the best description, or *ceque* in the terminology of the Spanish chroniclers. The lines are seen as paths between sacred places and most of them are not aligned astronomically. Maria Reiche found some astronomical alignments and Gerald Hawkins confirmed them, particularly the lines to the Pleiades and solar solstice. It is possible that these objects are among the host of random spirits venerated by the Indians.

The Indians possibly visited the *wak'as* in some kind of order, perhaps in turn either one after the other on a single day, or on a day-after-day basis. Possibly both. The order might have been learnt by rote, perhaps even counting from a solstice day: in this way a simple day-count calendar might have been created. The order might have been created by respecting dates on which ancestors died: dates that could not be directly related to the moon or stars. But most important of all were the spirits and the *wak'as* to which offerings and tokens were carried.

The meanings of the forms of the lines can only be speculative. Zigzags perhaps arose from making offerings to two rows of *wak'as*, the pious Indians moving alternately from one row to the next. Straight paths arose where principal *wak'as* were approached across lower, less important hills or as direct paths to holy places.

Straightness or directness was clearly of prime concern to the creators of the paths. The shortest distance between two *wak'as* had to be a straight line, but it was not always the easiest route. The paths were intended to be straight – Gerald Hawkins estimated they have a deviation of no more than four yards in a mile – and if, as seems most likely, the paths were pre-Spanish then the concept of straightness has to be an ancient one.

As yet no one has found a positive means of dating the paths and we can only speculate as to their age. Could the straight paths and *siq'is* have been an Inca concept? We know from the chroniclers that *ceques* and *wak'as* existed in Inca times though they did not mention paths as such, straight or otherwise. On the other hand they do talk of processions taking direct routes. More specifically, the chronicler Cristóbal Molina of Cuzco, describing the *capacocha*, a special sacrificial offering made to *wak'as* only in times of great need, writes that the children to be sacrificed were sent out 'not on the roads, but in a direct way over ravines and mountains'. Clearly, however, the chroniclers wrote mainly of the traditions of the Incas in Cuzco and the mountains, and we learn little from them of the customs of the coastal Indians.

The lines are generally thought to have been built sometime in the first thousand years A.D., but only on slim evidence. Gerald Hawkins's pottery traverse found sherds of all periods of the Nasca culture, but a preponderance of the style Nasca 3 on one line pointed to a construction date of around the first century A.D. (Of course these pots could have been placed or broken on the line at any time after their construction or just conceivably before.) The computer confirmed that the stone mounds and an eastern extension of Nasca's Great Rectangle would have aligned with Pleiades at A.D. 610, which closely corresponds with one Carbon 14 date of A.D. 525 (plus or minus eighty years) for a wooden post taken from the *pampa* (the exact location is not known and Carbon 14 dating techniques have improved since the 1950s).

These dates may match by chance but if not they may account for the very survival of the lines. If the lines had for some reason fallen into disuse in the pre-Inca period, they would have quickly appeared dull and obscure, as they are today – and thus become equally difficult to see. (But why they were not used in Inca times would need an explanation.) As the lines became difficult to distinguish on the ground, the Spanish priests probably never saw them, and anyway the Extirpation would not have been carried into the Nasca desert.

This obscurity would be true of all the other markings on the desert: the large cleared areas of so-called landing grounds, the rectangles and trapezoids, as well as the animal figures. And what of these? They do not fall easily into the scheme of a *ceque*, except as the flat areas described by Father Cobo as *wak'as* and places for gatherings. The Great Rectangle could be related to the Pleiades, the smaller one to the sun. But there are many cleared areas with no counterpart in the heavens. Again I believe the simple answer as outlined over thirty years ago by Dr Hans Horkheimer.

After visiting Nasca and Palpa in February and March 1946, Dr Horkheimer suggested the cleared areas were places for religious gatherings of Nascas, especially, he said, for ancestor worship. The size of the clearings varied according to the number of people using them and, like other ceremonial places in the desert region, they were built on ground not suitable for cultivation. Many of the *plazoletas* (little *plazas*), as Dr Horkheimer called them, were linked by lines to places which were sacred. Like Mejía Xesspe, the Peruvian archaeologist who, with Alfred Kroeber, first discovered the Nasca lines, Dr Horkheimer noticed that the main concentrations of the lines lay close to the valleys, often near the ancient burial grounds.

The spirals, of which Maria Reiche has counted more than a hundred, are often crossed by lines and seldom appear to be directly associated with them. Thus unless proof by dating is found, there is no reason to assume the spirals were part of the complex of ritual pathways.

It seems probable that most of the animal drawings preceded many of the lines, as so many lines cross the animals with apparent disregard for the designs and very few of the animals begin or end in a line. Unfortunately the places where a path-line and figure meet or cross have in many cases been disturbed by visitors. The early photographs taken by S.A.N. and Maria Reiche, together with the drawings of Mejía Xesspe, Alfred Kroeber and Hans Horkheimer, provide an irreplaceable record of the original state of the *pampa*, but it is impossible to date the features from these.

The animal figures are one of the most spectacular features of the *pampa*: they are very prolific and they have a characteristic style but, like the lines, they are not specific to Nasca. Other drawings of animals, circles and crowned men have been found and photographed on the Atacama desert in north Chile 480 miles to the south. They are undoubtedly representations of mythological gods and animal spirits and, if made by the Nascas, these spirits are likely to have belonged to the natural world around them. The Nascas might have seen the form of their gods in the configurations of some constellations, but without any clear-cut astronomical connection between the drawings and the stars, we have no proof. The *pista* and grid of the monkey drawing point only to one star and a faint one at that. The other lines there do not connect with a sky object. For the theory to be convincing that the animal figures represented constellations, lines drawn through all the thirty or so figures should be expected to point to stars and, as Gerald Hawkins reminds us, mostly they do not. The designs are probably no more than beautifully conceived iconography. Maria Reiche once said that 'all things on the *pampa* have a harmony and beauty, they have been made by people who were a kind of primitive intellectuals'.

The little 'men' figures on the hillsides at Nasca, with their peculiarly crowned heads, were simply made by clearing stones. They would not have required the careful measurement and planning devoted to the animal drawings. It is possible that they are of an earlier period, but that again must be conjecture.

When I arrived eventually in Nasca, the manager in the large reception office of the Turistas Hotel remembered me. He shook his head emphatically, as if he anticipated my question.

'The *Doctora* is on the *pampa*,' he said. Maria Reiche had left before dawn that day and it might be a week before she returned.

I knew Maria Reiche was still working on a unit of measurement which she believed had been used by the ancient people to construct the animal figures. The BBC team later filmed her demonstrating a method using string, taking the initial measurements from lengths of her own arms. She said she had discovered the ancient unit some years ago but, as she told me in Nasca, she had since revised the standard. The results of her research will be written down, she assured me, but only 'when certain calculations and proofs have been made'. The meticulous checking – comparing the efficacy of the unit against measurements of the many figures – now takes all her time.

Our long acquaintance had taught me that if the *Doctora* was working in the desert, she would not want to be interrupted, even supposing I could find her. So, checking out of the hotel early the next morning, I packed the car and headed north, once more towards Lima. For the first time I had no sense of regret at leaving the desolate *pampa*. Now I felt my work there had ended; that while many new puzzles had still to be solved, they would need the attention of specialists, especially archaeologists.

The morning was foggy and by 10.30 a.m. the sun had still not forced its way through the cloud. The desert, a grey, strangely cool and forbidding place, was lost in the mist within a mile of the road. When I stopped on the Pampa de San José, the metal observation tower stood skeleton-like and empty. The visitors would arrive when the weather cleared. A young watchman from Ingenio waited beside his small Japanese motor-cycle, ready to chase any vandals.

'The *Doctora*,' he said, 'is out there.' He waved his hand in the direction of Jumana, westwards across the silent *pampa*.

As long ago as 1954 Maria Reiche established her intention to devote her life to Nasca, either to prove or disprove the precise nature of Dr Kosok's giant 'astronomy book'. Her work is still concentrated towards this end. But while astronomy and mathematics are her main preoccupation, she has always had a broad appreciation of the *pampa*. She has always emphasized the vital importance of every single relic left on the *pampa* by the line builders. I now feel certain that archaeology and anthropology are the key disciplines in unravelling the mystery and that in exchange for lines and alignments, an incredible story will be read from other, less dramatic traces on the desert. Maria Reiche alone knows all the *pampa*, and her notes of finds such as stones, the coloured stone fragments, the ceramics and natural features hold clues for yet more exhaustive investigation in the fields other than astronomy.

The astronomical calendar hypothesis of Dr Kosok does not fit the computer findings of Gerald Hawkins on a one-line one-object basis. A few lines point to the winter and summer sun. The Great Rectangle might point to the Pleiades. Some lines might have been built to point in the general direction of constellations and other celestial objects perhaps including such features as the Magellanic Clouds, but these are large-angle, vague targets, and exact coupling cannot be proved mathematically.

The lines or paths might have belonged to or been cared for by individual families and, as Hans Horkheimer has said, they were very possibly constructed for ancestor worship. Neighbours or close kinship ties might account for long parallel lines to the same *wak'a*. The *wak'as* almost certainly represented spirits of ancestors and perhaps the mummies of the ancient Nascas were paraded in solemn ritual to the hills and other holy places. What libations, sacrifices and incantations were made can only be the subject of speculation. Of coloured stones (perhaps like those found on the Nasca *pampa* by Maria Reiche), Cristóbal de Albornoz says the Quechuas carried them in *chuspas* (little woven pouches) 'like the Christians have figures of saints they revere'. The coloured stones were called *auqui* and were offered to *wak'as*.

Whatever the rituals, they appear to have been made in remembrance of departed Nascas, whose remains once filled the burial grounds along the walls of the valleys. The lines as paths between the living and the dead form a vast, two-dimensional temple. Any traces of blood, coca, or ceremonial *chicha*, would have vanished from the surface in the past 2,000 years, washed away by intermittent rains which have undoubtedly struck the region. These have left only the stones and fragmented ceramic undisturbed, but each piece of pot, stone, chalk or sea shell, however small, is part of a saga which when told will re-create the people of the *pampa* once more. Maria Reiche has said that a temple does not exist on the desert, but long ago she suggested that the stone piles and cleared areas could have been sacred spots.

To extract the information from the desert will be as fascinating as it would be to release the secrets of a *quipu*. Indeed each line at Nasca is, I feel, remarkably like an early census computer tape, and carries an immensely detailed case history of the people who cared for the *wak'as* it linked. There might have been family paths, or paths belonging to a single kinship group. Other paths perhaps belonged to the entire community and were used by the whole population on days sacred to all the Nasca. I am sure the story is there.

But research takes time and many of the *pampa* features are deteriorating in the face of an onslaught of tourists. Already the *pampa* is guarded. Maria Reiche's ambition for the past thirty years has been total protection of the site. In 1955 as plans were made to irrigate the *pampa* and turn it into rich agricultural land, she hurried to Lima to fight single-handedly one of the bitterest conservation battles ever. At the time, the local papers declared resoundingly: 'Work threatening the Nasca Observatory has been halted.' Full scale protection is a costly undertaking and thankfully Peruvian archaeologists have taken the first steps.

If there is any heartfelt conclusion I have reached it concerns the clues on the ground. Information stored in a modern computer is easily erased, that is why it is expensively insured and protected. But the Nascas have gone and their unique data bank can be destroyed by turning a single stone or misplacing a tiny fragment of pot. Every design is distinctive, like the fingerprint of the artist who painted it. Each pot can be classified according to the valley it was made in, and eventually traced, right down to one man who died long ago beside that quiet desert in ancient America. Among the clues will be more representations of ancient beliefs, of spirits, strange beasts and forgotten gods. Our knowledge of legends and mythology is always incomplete, but somewhere, one day, someone may chance upon a detail, perhaps small and not immediately obvious, which will answer the question: 'Why so straight?'

The Nascas took great care to approach certain *wak'as* in direct paths and clearly the perfection was established as the paths were built. Over short distances on level ground the builders might have employed cords while poles and sighting marks would have been a simple procedure for long lines. The parallel paths would have been easy to mark off with measuring cords starting from the first line.

So the question remains not so much how, but why? Perhaps the ancient Nasca line-builders possessed the tidy mind of the surveyor, or did they have a deeper, more spiritual concern that made them struggle to mountain tops in the desert? Once, in the Andes, near Lake Titicaca, I asked an Indian about a route through the mountains. He gave me careful instructions that I was not to leave the path, as evil spirits hid everywhere. Though his concern might have stemmed from recent teaching, I believe it was old. The concept of special paths or routes to a divine place is not confined to one religion, and in Nasca the straightness of the paths is clearly demonstrable.

One legend of ancient gods, the Viracochas, perhaps older than Tiwanaku or Nasca, has become part of the Indian consciousness. The legend, like so many from the Andes, has obscure origins and one version of it may concern Nasca. I stumbled upon it almost by accident. After a long talk about *ceques* with archaeologist Mejía Xesspe, he confided: 'As a young man, I didn't like writing. I'd never have written down my theory of Nasca if Tello hadn't persuaded me.' But he showed me his research paper which concluded with a quotation from

Luis de Monzón, the magistrate who, in 1586, wrote of an old ruined village, worked stones and traces of ancient roads not far from present-day Nasca: 'The old Indians say that, by hearsay, they have knowledge of their ancestors, that in very old times, before the Incas ruled over them, there came to the land another people they call Viracochas, not many of them, and they were followed by Indians who came after them listening to their word, and now the Indians say they must have been saintly persons. And to them they built paths which can be seen today.'

It was less than a generation ago when the people of this isolated Andean village believed that spirits of ancestors dwelt at the top of the hill. After dancing in the square the Aymara went in procession to the shrines, making offerings on the way. The customs of the Nascas, whose graves pockmark the Peruvian desert, were never documented. Perhaps they used their paths for rituals? Perhaps.

Bibliography

Acosta, José de, *Historia Natural y Moral de las Indias* [1589], *Obras del P. José de Acosta de la Compañía de Jesus; estudio preliminar y edición del P. Francisco Mateos, Biblioteca de Autores Españoles*, tomo 73, pp. 1–247, Madrid: Ediciones Atlas, 1954.

Albornoz, Cristóbalde, 'La Instrucción para Descubrir Todas las Guacas del Pirú . . .', 1967. See Duviols.

Anonymous, *Discurso de la Sucesión y Gobierno de los Yngas*, ed. Victor M. Maurtua, in *Juicio de Limites entre el Perú y Bolivia, Prueba Peruana*, vol. 8, pp. 149–65, Madrid, 1906.

Arriaga, Pablo José de, *La Extirpación de la Idolatría del Pirú* [1621], ed. H. H. Urteaga and C. A. Romero, *Colección de Libros y Documentos Referentes a la Historia del Perú*, 2d ser., vol. 1, Lima, 1920.

Ascher, Marcia, and Ascher, Robert, 'The Quipu as a Visible Language', *Visible Language*, IX, 4, pp. 329–56, 1975.

Avila, Francisco de, *Dioses y Hombres de Huarochirí* [1608], traducción de José María Arquedas, Lima, 1966.

Bandelier, Adolph Francis, *The Islands of Titicaca and Koati*, New York: The Hispanic Society of America, 1910.

——, 'The Ruins at Tiahuanaco', *Proceedings American Antiquarian Society*, October 1911.

Bennett, Wendell, and Bird, Junius B., *Andean Culture History*, American Museum of Natural History, Handbook ser. 15, 1949.

Bertonio, Ludovico P., *Vocabulario de la Lengua Aymara* [1612], Edición Facsimilar, La Paz, Bolivia, 1956.

Betánzos, Juan de, *Suma y Narración de los Incas* [1551], ed. Marcos Jiménez de la Espada, *Biblioteca Hispano-Ultramarina*, vol 5, Madrid, 1880; *Biblioteca de Autores Españoles*, 209, 1–55, Madrid, 1968.

Brinckerhoff, Richard F., 'Astronomically-oriented Markings on Stonehenge', *Nature*, vol. 263, no. 5577, pp. 465–9, 7 October, 1976.

Broecker, W. S., Kulp, J. L., and Trucek, C. S., 'Lamont Natural
    Radiocarbon Measurements', III *Science*, vol. 124, no. 3213, pp.
    154–65, Washington D.C., 1956.
Bowman, Isaiah, *The Andes of Southern Peru: Geographical
    Reconnaissance Along the Seventy-Third Meridian*, American
    Geographical Society Special Publication no. 2, New York, 1916.
Bushnell, G. H. S., *Peru*, 'Ancient Peoples and Places Series', London:
    Thames & Hudson, 1956.
Calancha, Antonio de la, *Coronica Moralizada del Orden de San
    Augustin en el Perú*, Barcelona, 1638.
Casas, Bartolomé de las, 'Las Antiguas Gentes del Perú', 1559; *Col.
    Libr. Doc. Ref. Hist. Perú*, 1929.
Catholic Encyclopedia, The, 15 vols., New York, 1907–12.
Chávez Ballón, M., 'Cuidades Incas: Cuzco Capital del Imperio',
    Wayka, no. 3, Departamento de Antropología, Univ. Nac. del Cuzco,
    Peru, 1970.
Cieza de León, Pedro de, *Parte Primera de la Crónica del Perú*, Seville,
    1553.
——, *The Travels of Pedro Cieza de León*, trans. C. R. Markham,
    Hakluyt Society, 1 ser., 33, 1864.
——, *Segunda Parte de la Crónica del Perú, que trata del señorio de los
    Incas Yupanqui* [1554], trans. C. R. Markham, Hakluyt Society, 1
    ser., 68, 1883.
——, *The Incas of Pedro de Cieza de León* [combination of parts 1 and
    2], trans. Harriet de Onis, ed. Victor W. Von Hagen, Norman: Univ.
    of Oklahoma Press, 1959.
Clarke, R. M., 'A Calibration Curve for Radio Carbon Dates',
    Antiquity, XLIX, pp. 251–66, 1975.
Cobo, P. Bernabé, *Historia del Nuevo Mundo* [1653], ed. Marcos
    Jiménez de la Espada, Sociedad de Bibliófilos Andaluces, 4 vols.,
    Seville, 1890–95; ed. P. Francisco Mateos, *Biblioteca de Autores
    Españoles*, vols. XCI, XCII, Madrid, 1956.
Deuel, Leo, *Flights into Yesterday*, London: Macdonald, 1971.
Dumbarton Oaks, *Death and the Afterlife in Pre-Columbian America*, ed.
    Elizabeth P. Benson, Dumbarton Oaks Research Library and
    Collections, Washington D. C., 1973.
Duviols, Pierre, 'La Visite des Idolatries de Concepción de Chupas
    (Pérou 1614)', *Journal de la Société des Américanistes*, vol. 55, pp.
    497–510, Paris, 1966.

——, 'Un Inédit de Cristóbal de Albornoz: La Instrucción para Descubrir Todas las Guacas del Pirú y sus Camayos y Haziendas', *Journal de la Société des Américanistes*, vol. 56, Paris, 1967.

Garcilaso de la Vega, 'el Inca', *Comentarios Reales de los Incas* [1604], Edición al cuidado de Angel Rosenblat, segunda edición, Buenos Aires: Emecé Editores, 1945.

——, *Royal Commentaries of the Incas*, trans. Harold V. Livermore, Texas Pan American Series, Austin & London, 1966.

Gerster, Georg, 'Ein Bilderbuch, für Götter?', *Geo*, no. 7, Hamburg, 1977.

Gonçález Holguín, Diego, *Vocabulario de la Lengua General de Todo el Perú Llamada Lengua Quinchua, o del Inca . . .*, Lima, 1608; Edición del Instituto de Historia, Universidad Nacional Mayor de San Marcos, Lima, 1952.

Gregory, Herbert E., 'A Geographical Reconnaissance of the Cuzco Valley, Perú', *American Journal of Science*, 4th ser., vol. 41, no. 241, pp. 1–100, 1916.

Gross, Daniel R., *Peoples and Cultures of Native South America*, New York: Doubleday/The Natural History Press, 1973.

Guamán Poma de Ayala – see Poma de Ayala.

Handbook of South American Indians, ed. Julian H. Steward, vol. 2, *The Andean Civilizations*, Smithsonian Institution, Bureau of American Ethnology Bulletin 143, Washington D. C., 1963.

Hawkins, Gerald S., *Ancient Lines in the Peruvian Desert*, Smithsonian Institution Astrophysical Observatory, Cambridge, Mass., 1969.

——, *Beyond Stonehenge*, New York: Harper & Row; London: Hutchinson (Arrow Books, 1977), 1973.

——, *Astronomical Alinements in Britain, Egypt, and Peru*, Smithsonian Institution Astrophysical Observatory, Cambridge, Mass., 1973; *Trans. of Royal Society of London*, vol. 276, no. 1257, p. 157, 1974.

——, 'Astro-archaeology: Scientific Knowledge Shown by Prehistoric Man', *Pears Cyclopaedia*, 82nd ed., pp. F60–F62, London, 1973.

——, 'Prehistoric Markings in Peru', National Geographic Society, *Research Reports* 1967 *Projects*, pp. 117–44, Washington D.C., 1974.

——, 'Astro-archaeology: The Unwritten Evidence', in *Archaeoastronomy*, ed. A. Aveni, New Haven: Yale University Press, pp. 131–62, 1975.

——, 'Stargazers of the Ancient World', *Encycl. Britannica Yearbook*, 'Science and the Future', pp. 124–37, 1976.

Hawkins, Gerald S., and Rosenthal, S. K., '5000- and 10,000-year Star Catalogs', *Smithsonian Contr. Astrophys.*, vol. 10, no. 2., pp. 141–79, 1967.

Hawkins, Gerald S., and White, J. B., *Stonehenge Decoded*, New York: Doubleday, 1965; London: Souvenir Press, 1966.

Hernández Príncipe, Rodrigo, 'Mitología Andina', ed. C. A. Romero, *Inca*, vol. 1, no. 1, pp. 25–68, 1923.

Horkheimer, Hans, 'Las Plazoletas, Rayas y Figuras Prehispánicas en las Pampas y Crestas de la Hoya del Río Grande', *Revista del a Universidad Nacional de Trujillo*, Epoca II, no. 1, pp. 45–63, 1947.

——, 'Identificación y Bibliografía de Importantes Sitios Prehispánicos del Perú, *Arqueólogicas*, no. 8, Museo Nacional de Antropología y Arqueología, Lima, 1955.

Hoyle, Fred, 'Stonehenge – An Eclipse Predictor', *Nature*, vol. 211, pp. 454–6, 1966.

——, *On Stonehenge*, London: Heinemann Educational, 1977.

Kaufmann, Doig, Federico, *El Perú Arqueólogico*, Lima: Grafis, 1976.

Kosok, Paul, 'The Mysterious Markings of Nazca', *Natural History*, vol. 56, pp. 200–7, May 1947.

——, 'Pre-Inca Markings in Peru', *Life*, vol. 23, pp. 75–6, July 1947.

——, 'Desert Puzzle of Peru', *Science Illustrated*, pp. 60–1, September 1947.

——, *Life, Land and Water in Ancient Peru*, Brooklyn: Long Island University Press, 1965.

Kosok, Paul, and Reiche, Maria, 'Ancient Drawings on the Desert of Peru', *Archaeology*, vol. 2, December, pp. 206–15, 1949.

La Barre, Weston, *The Aymara Indians of the Lake Titicaca Plateau, Bolivia*, Memoir no. 68, Washington D.C.: American Anthropological Association, 1948.

Lancho Rojas, Josue, *Ensayo Histórico de Nasca*, Lima: Editorial EUSA 1974.

Lehmann-Nitsche, R., 'Coricancha', *Revista del Museo de la Plata*, vol. 7, ser. 3, pp. 1–256, 1928.

Lumbreras, Luis G., *De los Pueblos, los Culturas y las Artes del Antiguo Perú*, Lima, 1969.

Lynch, Thomas F., *The Antiquity of Man in South America*, Cornell University Latin American Studies Program, Reprint No. 53, from *Quarternary Research*, vol. 4, no. 3, September 1974.

McIntyre, Loren, 'Mystery of the Ancient Nazca Lines', *National Geographic Magazine*, vol. 147, no. 5, pp. 716–28, 1975.

Masson, Duncan, 'Those Nasca Lines', *Lima Times*, July, pp. 7–11, 1976.

Matienzo, Juan de, *Gobierno del Perú* [1567], ed. J. N. Matienzo, Buenos Aires, 1910; ed. G. Lohmann Villena, Paris and Lima, 1967.

Means, Philip Ainsworth, 'Biblioteca Andina', *Transactions of the Connecticut Academy of Arts and Sciences*, vol. 29, pp. 271–525, May 1928.

Medina, Felipe, 'Relación del Licenciado Felipe de Medina, Visitador General de las Idolatrías de Arzobispado de Lima, enviada al Ilustrisimo y Reverendísimo Sr. Arzobispo della, en que le da Cuenta de las que se han Descubierto en el Pueblo de Huacho, donde ha Comenzado a Visitar, desde 19 de Febrero hasta 23 de Marzo de 1650', *Col. Libr. Doc. Ref. Hist. Perú*, tomo III, 2 serie, pp. 89–102, Peru, 1920.

Mejía Xesspe, Toribio, 'Costumbres Indígenas, Región Andina', *Inca*, vol. 1, no. 4, pp. 884–903, 1923.

——, 'Acueductos y Caminos Antiquos de la Hoya del Río Grande de Nasca', *Actos y Trabajos Científicos*, pp. 559–70, 27th International Conference of Americanists, Lima, vol. 1, 1939.

Menzel, Dorothy, 'The Inca Occupation of the South Coast of Peru', *South-western Journal of Anthropology*, 15(2), pp. 125–42, 1959.

——, *The Archaeology of Ancient Peru and the Work of Max Uhle*, R. H. Lowie Museum of Anthropology, University of California, Berkeley, 1977.

Mercado de Peñalosa, Pedro, 'Relación de la Provincia de los Pacajes', *Relaciones Geográficas de Indias* [1586], tomo 2, pp. 51–64, Madrid, 1881–97.

Metraux, Alfred, 'Contribution au Folk-lore Andin', *Journal de la Société des Américanistes*, Paris, vol. 26, pp. 67–103, 1934.

——, 'L'Organisation Sociale et les Survivances Religieuses des Indiens Uro-Čipaya de Carangas (Bolivie)', *International Congress of Americanists*, sess. 25, La Plata, 1932, vol. 1, pp. 191–213, 1934.

——, 'Civilización Material de los Indios Uro-Čipaya de Carangas (Bolivia)', *Revista del Instituto de Antropología de la Universidad Nacional de Tucuman*, Argentina, vol. 3, entr. 1a. pp. 85–129, 1935.

——, 'Les Indiens Uro-Chipaya de Carangas: Avant-propos', *Journal de la Société des Américanistes*, Paris, vol. 27, pp. 111–28, 1935.

——, 'Les Indiens Uro-Čipaya de Carangas: La Religion', *Journal de la Société des Américanistes*, Paris, vol. 27, pp. 325–415, 1935.

241

———, 'Les Indiens Uro-Čipaya de Carangas: La Civilisation Matérielle', *Journal de la Société des Américanistes*, Paris, vol. 28, pp. 155–207, 1936.

Molina (of Cuzco), Cristóbal de, 'Relación de las Fábulas y Ritos de los Incas' [1575], *Los Pequeños Grandes Libros de Historia Americana*, serie I, tomo IV, 2nd paging., Lima: D. Miranda, 1934.

Monzón, Luis de, *Relaciones Geográficas de Indias* [1586], tomo 4, p. 120, Madrid, 1881–97.

Müller, Rolf, 'Die Intiwatana (Sonnenwarten) im Alten Peru', *Baessler-Archiv*, Band XIII, Berlin, pp. 178–87, 1929.

———, 'Der Sonnentempel in den Ruinen von Tihuanacu. Versuch einer astronomischen Altersbestimmung', *Baessler-Archiv*, Band XIV, Berlin, pp. 123–42, 1930–31.

Murúa (Morúa), Martín de, 'Historia del Origen y Genealogía Real de los Reyes Incas del Perú, de sus Hechos, Costumbres, Trajes y Manera De Gobierno' [c. 1605], ed. H. H. Urteaga and C. A. Romero, *Col. Libr. Doc. Ref. Hist. Perú*, 2a serie, vol. 4, pp. 1–253; vol. 5, pp. 1–72, Lima, 1922–5.

Nordenskiöld, Erland, 'Calculations with Years and Months in the Peruvian *Quipus*', *Comparative Ethnographical Studies*, Gothenburg Museum, vol. 6, part 2, 1925.

———, 'The Secret of the Peruvian *Quipus*', *Comparative Ethnographical Studies*, Gothenburg Museum, vol. 6, part 1, 1925.

Orbigny, Alcide D', *Voyage dans l'Amérique Méridionale*, vols. 2 and 4 (9 vols.), Paris, 1835–47.

———, *Voyage dans les Deux Amériques*, Paris, 1867.

Osborne, H., *Indians of the Andes*, London: Routledge & Kegan Paul, 1952.

Paredes, M. Rigoberto, *Mitos, Supersticiones y Supervivencias Populares de Bolivia*, segunda edición, La Paz: Atenea, 1936.

Pease, G. V. Franklin, *El Dios Creador Andino*, Lima, 1973.

Pelikan, Ted, 'The Cantogrande Valley', *Peruvian Times*, 26 April, 1968.

Perez Bocanegra, Juan, *Ritual Formulario; e Institución de Cura, para Administrar a los Naturales de Este Reyno . . .'*, Lima, 1631.

Pezzia Assereto, Alejandro, *La Cultura Nazca*, Lima, 1962.

———, *Guía del Mapa Arqueológico-pictográfico del Departamento de Ica*, Lima: Editora Italperú, 1970.

———, *El Rayado Descomunal Nazquense*, Instituto Nacional de Cultura Oficina Departamental, Ica, 1976.

Polo de Ondegardo, Juan, 'Report by Polo de Ondegardo. The Rites and Laws of the Incas', trans. and ed. R. Markham, Hakluyt Society, pp. 151–71, London, 1873.

——, 'Los Errores y Supersticiones de los Indios, Sacadas del Tratado y Averiguación que Hizo el Licenciado Polo', ed. H. H. Urteaga and C. A. Romero, *Col. Libr. Doc. Ref. Hist. Perú.* 1st ser., vol. 3, pp. 1–43, 1916.

Poma de Ayala, Felipe Guamán, 'Nueva Corónica y Buen Gobierno' [1613], *Institut d'Ethnologie, Travaux et Mémoires*, Paris, vol. 23, 1936.

Ponce Sangines, Carlos, *Tunupa y Ekako. Estudio Arqueológico Acerca de las Efigies Precolombinas de Dorso Adunco*, Academia Nacional de Ciencias de Bolivia, La Paz, Publicación no. 20, 1969.

——, *Puma Punku. Procedencia de las Areniscas Utilizadas en el Templo Pre-Colombino de Puma Punku*, Academia Nacional de Ciencias de Bolivia, La Paz, Publicación no. 22, 1971.

——, *Tiwanaku*, Academia Nacional de Ciencias de Bolivia, La Paz, Publicación no. 30, 1972.

Porras Barrenechea, Raúl, *Fuentes Históricas Peruanas*, Juan Mejía Baca y P. L. Villanueva, editores, Lima, 1954.

Posnansky, Arthur, *Guía General Illustrada para la Investigación de los Monumentos Prehistóricas de Tiahuanaco é Islas del Sol y la Luna (Titicaca y Koaty)*, La Paz, Bolivia, 1912.

——, 'Los Urus o Uchumi', *Congreso Internacional de Americanistas*, sess. 25, La Plata, 1932, vol. 1, pp. 234–300, 1934.

——, *Tiahuanacu: The Cradle of American Man*, New York, 1945.

Ramos de Cox, Josefina, *Informe Elevado al Patronato de Arqueología*, Lima, 2 November, 1971.

Reiche, Maria, *Los Dibujos Gigantescos en el Suelo de las Pampas de Nazca y Palpa*. Lima, 1949.

——, *Mystery on the Desert: A New Revelation of Ancient Peru*, Lima, 1949.

——, 'Prehistoric Ground Drawings in Peru', *Photographie und Forschung: The Contax in the Service of Science*, Zeiss Ikon, Stuttgart, 1954.

——, 'Vorgeschichtliche Bodenzeichnungen in Peru', *Die Umschau in Wissenschaft und Technik*, 55 Jahrgang, Heft II, pp. 332–4, 1955.

——, 'Interpretación Astronómica de la Figura del Mono en la Pampa al sur del Río Ingenio', Centro de Estudios Históricos Militares del Perú, *Actos y Trabajos del II Congreso Nacional del Historia del Perú*, Lima, pp. 285–6, 1958.

———, 'El Pájaro Anunciador del Inti Raymi', *Cultura y Pueblo* II, 6, Lima, 1965.

———, *Geheimnis der Wüste – Mystery on the Desert – Secreto de la Pampa*, Stuttgart, 1968.

———, 'Giant Ground Drawings on the Peruvian Desert, *Verhandlungen des XXVIII Internationalen Amerikanistenkongresses*, Stuttgart-München *12–18.8.1968*, Bd. 1, pp. 379–84, 1968.

———, Rätselbilder in der Wüste', *Hobby*, no. 9, April 1969, pp. 66–75.

———, 'How the Nazca Lines were Made', *Peruvian Times*, Lima, April 1973, pp. 9–13.

———, 'Las Gigantescas Huellas de Nazca y Palpa', *Imagen*, no. 3, (May), Lima, 1974.

———, *Peruvian Ground Drawings*, Munich: Kunstraum, 1974.

Relación de la Religión y Ritos del Perú, ed. H. H. Urteaga, *Col. Libr. Doc. Ref. Hist. Perú*, vol. II, pp. 3–56, Lima, 1918.

Relaciones Geográficas de Indias, Peru, Madrid: Marcos Jiménez de la Espada, 4 vols., 1881–97.

Rossel Castro, Alberto, 'Figuras Geométricas Prehistóricas de la Hoya de Río Grande de Nasca', Centro de Estudios Históricos Militares del Perú, *Actos y Trabajos del II Congreso Nacional del Historia del Perú*, Lima, pp. 351–9, 1958.

Rostworowski de Diez Canseco, María, 'Las Etnías del Valle del Chillón', *Revista del Museo Nacional*, tomo XXXVIII, Lima, 1972.

———, 'El Sitio Arqueológico de Concon, en el Valle del Chillón: derrotero etnohistórico', *Revista del Museo Nacional*, tomo XXXVIII, Lima, 1972.

———, *Los Ayarmacas*, Casa Museo de Colón, Lima, 1975.

———, *Etnía y Sociedad*, Instituto de Estudios Peruanos, Lima, 1977.

Rowe, John Howland, 'An Introduction to the Archeology of Cuzco', *Papers of the Peabody Museum of American Archaeology and Ethnology, Harvard University*, vol. XXVII, no. 2, Cambridge, Mass., 1944.

———, 'Absolute Chronology in the Andean Area', *American Antiquity*, vol. 10, no. 3, pp. 265–84, 1945.

———, 'Inca Culture at the Time of the Spanish Conquest', *Handbook of South American Indians*, vol. 2, pp. 183–330; Smithsonian Institution Bureau of American Ethnology, *Bulletin 143*, Washington D.C., 1946.

———, 'Archaeological Explorations in Southern Peru 1954–1955', *American Antiquity*, vol. 22, no. 2, pp. 135–50, Salt Lake City, 1956.

———, 'What Kind of Settlement was Inca Cuzco?', *Ñawa Pacha*, 5, pp. 59–76, Institute of Andean Studies, University of California, Berkeley, 1967.

Rowe, John Howland, and Menzel, Dorothy, *Peruvian Archaeology: Selected Readings*, Palo Alto: Peek Publications, 1967.

Santa-Cruz Pachacuti Yamqui, Juan de, 'Relación de Antiguedades desde Reyno del Perú' [1613], *Col. Libr. Doc. Ref. Hist. Perú*, tomo IX, 2 serie, 1927.

Sarmiento de Gamboa, Pedro, 'Historia dé los Incas' [1572], *Biblioteca Emecé de Obras Universales*, Sección X, *Historia y Arqueología*, no. 85, tercera edición, Buenos Aires,: Emecé Editores, 1947.

Squier, Ephraim George, *Peru: Incidents of Travel and Exploration in the Land of the Incas*, New York: Harper Brothers, 1877.

Strong, William Duncan, 'Paracas, Nazca and Tiahuanacoid Cultural Relationships in South Coastal Peru', *American Antiquity*, vol. XXII, no. 4, part 2, 1957.

Tejeiro, Antonio, 'El Cielo de la Paz', *La Paz en su IV Centenario*, tomo 1, La Paz, 1948.

Trimborn, Hermann, *El Motivo Explanatorio en los Mitos de Huarochiri*, Letras Universidad Nacional Mayor de San Marcos, Lima, 1955.

Tschopik, Jr., Harry, 'The Aymara', *Handbook of South American Indians*, vol. 2: *The Andean Civilizations*, Bulletin, Bureau of American Ethnology, no. 143, pp. 501–73, Smithsonian Institution, Washington D.C., 1946.

———, 'The Aymara of Chucuito, Peru, I: Magic', *Anthropological Papers of the American Museum of Natural History*, vol. 44, part 2, New York, 1951.

Uhle, Max, 'The Nazca Pottery of Ancient Peru', *Proceedings of the Davenport Academy of Sciences*, vol. 13, pp. 1–16, Davenport, Iowa, 1914.

Urteaga, Horacio H., 'Observatorios Astronómicos de los Incas', *Boletín de la Sociedad Geográfica de Lima*, vol. 29, pp. 40–6, 1913.

Valera, Blas, 'Relación de las Costumbres Antiguas de los Naturales del Pirú', ed. Marcos Jiménez de la Espada, *Tres Relaciones de Antigüedades Peruanas*, pp. 135–227, Madrid, 1879.

Vasquez de Espinosa, Antonio, 'Compendium and Description of the West Indies', *Smithsonian Miscellaneous Collections*, vol. 102. 1942.

Wachtel, Nathan, *Vision of the Vanquished*, Hassocks, Sussex: Harvester Press, 1977.

Waisbard, Simone, *Les Pistes de Nasca,* Paris: Laffont, 1977.

Wallace, Dwight, 'Ceremonial Roads in Chincha: Symbolic and Political Implications', Paper presented at the 1977 SAA symposium: Commodity Flow and Political Development in the Andes, New Orleans, 1977.

Willey, G. S., *Introduction to American Archaeology,* vol. 2, *South America,* Englewood Cliffs, N.J.: Prentice-Hall, 1972.

Zárate, Augustín de, 'Historia del Descubrimiento y Conquista de la Provincia del Perú', *Biblioteca de Autores Españoles,* vol. 26, pp. 459–574, 1853.

Zuidema, R. T., *The Ceque System of Cuzco,* International Archives of Ethnography, E. J. Brill, Leiden, 1964.

——, 'El Calendario Inca', *Actas y Memorias XXXVI Congreso International de Americanistes,* Seville, vol. 2, pp. 25–30, 1966.

——, 'Meaning in Nasca Art. Iconographic Relationships between Inca-, Huari-, and Nazca cultures in Southern Peru', *Arstryck,* pp. 35–54, Goteborgs Etnografiska Museum, Gothenburg, 1971.

——, Kinship and Ancestorcult in Three Peruvian Communities; Hernandez Principé's Account in 1622', *Bulletin Institut Français des Etudes Andines,* vol. II, no. 1, pp. 16–33, Lima, 1973.

——, 'La Imagen del Sol y la Huaca de Susurpuquio en el Sistema Astronómico de los Incas en el Cuzco', *Journal de la Société des Américanistes,* vol. 63, pp. 199–230, Paris, 1974.

Zuidema, R. T., and Quispe, U., 'A Visit to God: The Account and Interpretation of a Religious Experience in the Peruvian Community of Choque-Huarcaya', *Bijdragen Tot de Taal, Land-en-Volkenkunde,* vol. 124, pp. 22–39, 1968.

Hawkins, Gerald S., *Beyond Stonehenge*, New York: Harper & Row; London: Hutchinson (Arrow Books, 1977), 1973.

Hemming, John, *The Conquest of the Incas*, London: Macmillan; New York: Harcourt, Brace, 1970.

Howell, Mark, *Journey Through a Forgotten Empire*, London: Bles, 1964.

Kendall, Ann, *Everyday Life of the Incas*, new ed., London: Batsford; New York: Putnam, 1973.

McIntyre, Loren, *The Incredible Incas and Their Timeless Land*, National Geographic Society, 1975.

Mason, J. Alden, *The Ancient Civilizations of Peru*, rev. ed., London: Penguin Books, 1969.

Osborne, Harold, *South American Indian Mythology*, London: Hamlyn, 1968.

Von Hagen, V. W., *Highway of the Sun*, New York, 1956.

Acknowledgements

Tony and Marion Morrison wish to thank the following for help in preparing this book and the two films:

Nicholas Asheshov, Lima; Esther Ashton de Bonilla, La Paz; Adolfo Bermudez Jenkins, Ica, Peru; Nilda Cáceres, M.B.E., Lima; Dan and Gisela Carter, Lima; David and Yvette Cole, Paris; Jenny Cooper, London; Juan de Dios Yapita, La Paz; Margot Gentile, Lima; Dr. Eufronio Gonzalez E., La Paz; David Goodfellow, London; Eleanor Griffis, Lima; Herman Kanaviri, Machacamarca, Bolivia; Mrs. Theodora Kroeber-Quinn, Berkeley; Josue Lancho, Nasca; Alfredo LaPlaca, La Paz; Hazel Lewis, London; Dr. Hugo Ludeña, Lima; Philip and Dorothy Maclean, New York; Cancio Mamani Lopez, La Paz; Brigida Martino, Brussels; Jackie Matthews, London; Mrs. Alexandra Morgan, Vienna; Ted Pelikan, Miami; John and Mary Penney, London; Teniente O. Pericon, La Paz; Alejandro Pezzia Assereto, Ica, Peru; Dora Prada de Pezzia, Ica Peru; Tristan Platt, La Paz; Dr. Franz Ressel, Mannheim; Eduardo Ronalds Dogny, Lima; Steve Rocketto, Connecticut; Cathy Sachs, Washington; Keith Sheehan, London.

Index